Kinship, Friendship, Sex, and Aggression in Free-ranging Rhesus Monkeys

by

Andrew Peter Wilson

Previously Titled:

Social Behavior of Free-ranging Rhesus Monkeys with an Emphasis on Aggression

PhD thesis in Anthropology, UC Berkeley, August 1968

Social Behavior of Free-ranging Rhesus Monkeys with an

Emphasis on Aggression

by

Andrew Peter Wilson

A.B. (University of Michigan) 1963

DISSERTATION

Submitted in partial satisfaction of the requirements for the degree of

DOCTOR OF PHILOSOPHY

in

Anthropology

in the

GRADUATE DIVISION

of the

UNIVERSITY OF CALIFORNIA, BERKELEY

August 1968

Approved by Professor Sherwood L. Washburn

Professor George Barlow

Professor Phyllis Jay

TO ANGEL FIGUEROA,

WITH GRATITUDE

PREFACE

As an undergraduate, my interest in the physical and behavioral evolution of man was influenced by Professors Marston Bates, Frank B. Livingstone, Leslie A. White, and Eric R. Wolf at the University of Michigan, and Morris Goodman and Gabriel Lasker at Wayne State University.

As a graduate student at the University of California, problems concerning the relationship of nonhuman primate social behavior to the understanding of man's social origins were pointed out to me by Professor Sherwood L. Washburn. It was largely his intellectual stimulation, advice, and support which made this research possible.

Professor J. Desmond Clark sat on the committee for my oral examination. His discourses with me on African prehistory provided an important link in my chain of thought for understanding the transition between ape and human society. The lectures of Professor Theodore D. McCown provided a critical and analytical synthesis of human prehistory.

Professor James N. Anderson and I spent many interesting hours discussing the relationships between human and animal ecology. He also served as chairman of my orals committee.

Professor Phyllis Jay influenced me by her writings on primate behavior and served on my orals and thesis committees.

Professor Peter Marler taught me about animal behavior and impressed upon me the necessity of considering both endogenous and exogenous factors when attempting to explain behavior. He also participated in my oral examination.

Professor George W. Barlow served on my thesis committee.

Professor Donald Stone Sade introduced me to Cayo Santiago and field work with monkeys. His companionship and tutelage were invaluable.

My research at Cayo Santiago was conducted with the permission of the National Institutes of Health, National Institute of Neurological Diseases and Blindness, Laboratory of Perinatal Physiology, San Juan, Puerto Rico. Drs. Ronald E. Myers, John A. Morrison, and C. P. Swett facilitated my study in every way possible. Mr. Angel Figueroa, animal caretaker, shared with me his unparalleled knowledge of the Cayo Santiago rhesus monkeys.

Dr. Carl Koford sent me information on individual monkeys at Cayo Santiago.

Mrs. Alice Davis facilitated my contacts between Puerto Rico and Berkeley while I was in the field.

My wife, Sonia, has been a constant source of help and encouragement.

Statistical aid was provided by Mr. Lawrence W. Ribnick.

Financial support for this study was provided by the United States Public Health Service, Grant Numbers GM-1224 and MH-08623, and a grant-in-aid from the Department of Anthropology, University of California, Berkeley.

I thank all these individuals and institutions for their kindness and help in making this research possible.

Berkeley, California
July 1968

ABSTRACT

A fourteen-month, 1400-hour study of free-ranging rhesus monkeys (Macaca mulatta) was made at the Cayo Santiago island colony in Puerto Rico. The primary topics of study were (1) nocturnal behavior, (2) seasonal fluctuations in aggression and social dominance and their relationship to reproduction, and (3) intergroup relations with an emphasis on male intergroup transfer.

Nocturnal behavior. Social groups of monkeys slept almost exclusively in well-defined sleeping areas on the leeward side of the island, although the exact location of any one group at night was highly variable. Increased agonistic activity was noted to be most intense just before dark, when the groups climbed into the trees to sleep. On nights with bright moonlight, the monkeys often came to the ground and engaged in typical daylight activities, such as fighting and copulation. Sleeping postures and the ascent and descent from the trees were described.

Seasonal fluctuations in aggression and social dominance and their relationship to reproduction. Aggression was seen to fluctuate seasonally. Wounds and month of death were followed over a two-year period. Deaths and wounds were correlated with the mating season (July-December) for male monkeys, but not for females. Changes of dominance rank occurred more often in the mating season in both males and females. Confinement of the birth season to the period of least aggression was discussed in terms of adaptive value to the population, and related to seasonal fluctuations of aggression of rhesus monkeys in India.

Intergroup relations with an emphasis on male intergroup transfer. The following topics were discussed: agonistic intergroup relations, the relationship of grooming and association to nonagonistic social relations, nonagonistic intergroup relations, intergroup male transfer, the integration of males into a new group, and the significance of intergroup male transfer for intergroup social relations. Long-term affectional ties were seen to play a part in the intergroup transfer of male monkeys.

CONTENTS

Page

PREFACE iv

ABSTRACT vi

CHAPTER

   I. INTRODUCTION 1

      A. Justification 1
      B. Behavioral Studies of Free-ranging Rhesus Monkeys . . 2
      C. The Facilities at Cayo Santiago 3
      D. Materials, Methods, and Aims 4
      E. Group Composition 9
      F. Dispersion of Groups 11
      G. Diurnal Activity Patterns 13

  II. NOCTURNAL BEHAVIOR 16

      A. Introduction 16
      B. Methods 16
      C. Dispersion of Groups at Night 17
      D. Progression of Groups to Sleeping Areas 19
      E. Increased Agonistic Behavior at Dusk 20
      F. Effects of Moonlight on Nocturnal Activity 21
      G. Sleeping Positions, Ascent and Descent from the Trees 21
      H. Discussion 24

 III. SEASONAL FLUCTUATIONS IN AGGRESSION AND SOCIAL DOMINANCE
     AND THEIR RELATIONSHIP TO REPRODUCTIVE BEHAVIOR 29

      A. Introduction 29
      B. Methods Used in Determining Dominance Status 29
      C. Female Dominance 35
      D. Male Dominance 39
      E. Seasonal Fluctuations in Wounds 57
      F. Seasonal Fluctuations in Mortality 59
      G. Discussion 62

  IV. INTERGROUP RELATIONS WITH AN EMPHASIS ON MALE INTERGROUP
     TRANSFER 66

      A. Introduction 66
      B. Agonistic Intergroup Behavior 66
      C. The Relationship of Grooming and Association to
         Nonagonistic Social Relations 70
      D. Nonagonistic Intergroup Relations 72
      E. Intergroup Male Transfer 78

CHAPTER   Page

    F.   Integration of Males into a New Group   81
    G.   The Significance of Intergroup Male Transfer for
           Intergroup Social Relations   83
    H.   Discussion   86

APPENDIX   88

   A.   Tables 24-27   89

   B.   A Catalogue of Agonistic and Affectional Behavior   99

REFERENCES   126

LIST OF TABLES

Table   Page

1. Comparison of Sleeping Subgroup Size 27

2. Dominance Interactions Between Females of Two Female Lines in Group J 37

3. Relationship of Number of Monkeys in Female Line to Line Dominance 38

4. Dominance Interactions Between Sisters 40

5. Dyadic Dominance Interactions in Group A 41

6. Dyadic Dominance Interactions in Group C 45

7. Dyadic Dominance Interactions in Group E 46

8. Dyadic Dominance Interactions in Group F 47

9. Dyadic Dominance Interactions in Group H 48

10. Dyadic Dominance Interactions in Group I 49

11. Dyadic Dominance Interactions in Group J 50

12. Dominance Interactions in Which Coalitions Were Observed . 51

13. Changes in Dominance Rank of Ten Highest Ranking Males in Group A from June 1962 to August 1967 52

14. Observed Changes in Male Dominance Status 54

15. Triangular Dominance Relationships of Males 58

16. Wound Frequencies by Month 60

17. Mortality by Month 61

18. Supplanting Interactions Between Identified Groups 67

19. Intergroup Individual Dominance Interactions 69

20. Groups Sitting Within 20 Feet of Each Other 75

21. Changes in Group Membership 80

22. Male Associations 84

23. Proportion and Percentage of Males in Each Group Born in the Group of Membership 85

Table   Page

24. Monkeys Removed from Cayo Santiago (Aug. 1965 -
     Aug. 1967)   89

25. Monkeys Found Dead at Cayo Santiago (Aug. 1965 -
     Aug. 1967)   90

26. Census, August 1965   91

27. Census, August 1967   95

28. Aggressive Displays and Behavior Patterns   101

29. Submissive Displays and Behavior Patterns   103

30. Affectional Displays and Behavior Patterns   104

31. Agonistic Play   104

LIST OF ILLUSTRATIONS

Figure   Page

1. Map of Cayo Santiago 5

2. Photographs of Cayo Santiago 6

3. Photographs of Feeders and Traps 7

4. Population Changes Since 1956 10

5. Sleeping Areas 18

6. Battle Line Formation 108

7. Broadside Display 111

"Most sorts of diversion in men, children, and other animals, are an imitation of fighting."

Jonathan Swift, 1706

I. INTRODUCTION

A. Justification

A number of publications and symposia have attempted to lay the foundations for the scientific study of human aggression (Collias 1944, de Reuck and Knight 1966, Freeman 1964, Hall 1964, Kourilsky, Soulairac, and Grapin 1965, Washburn 1966, Washburn and Hamburg 1968). In recent years, scientists concentrating on animal behavior have collaborated with behavioral scientists in an effort to gain a better understanding of the biological basis of human conflict (Carthy and Ebling 1964). Social scientists have pointed out the relevance of animal behavior to the study of aggression in man (Tiger and Fox 1966, Brown 1967), as have ethologists (Lorenz 1964) and comparative psychologists (Scott 1958, 1962).

While aggression receives a great deal of attention from these researchers, who synthesized data from animal and human behavior, an appreciation for the role of affectional bonds and cooperation in the control and expression of such potentially disruptive behavior is also recognized. Allee (1951), Lorenz (1966), and Etkin (1964) have noted that, particularly among social animals, intraspecific aggression is often closely related to affectional ties.

In my study of the rhesus monkeys at Cayo Santiago it was impossible to understand their aggressive behavior without carefully considering their affectional relations as well. Indeed, it is probable that although aggression and affection in both human and nonhuman primates appear superficially to be diametrically opposed aspects of behavior, they are, in fact, closely linked.

While the study of aggression in <u>Macaca</u> <u>mulatta</u> is a step toward understanding the behavior of other species of nonhuman primates, it is also relevant to understanding human behavior. I believe that the perspective of evolutionary theory which stresses comparative studies of phylogenetically related species is basic to the study of social behavior by anthropologists as well as ethologists. Of course, the study of human behavior involves problems different from those involved in studying the behavior of nonhuman primates just as the study of fish or insect behavior involves techniques which may not suffice for elephants (Hinde and Tinbergen 1958). However, we should not expect <u>Homo</u> <u>sapiens</u> to be without any behavioral adaptations in common with other vertebrate species, particularly with members of his own order, the Primates. Learned behavior (particularly culture), as important as it may be for human social life, cannot be uninfluenced by a genetic predisposition to be more easily shaped in certain ways than in others. Thus, hopefully, the study of nonhuman primate behavior may help in integrating ethological research into the study of human social life.

B. <u>Behavioral Studies of Free-ranging Rhesus Monkeys</u>

The rhesus monkey has recently been the focus of several excellent studies concerned with its ecology and behavior in its native habitat, India. Southwick (1962), Southwick and Beg (1961), Southwick, Beg and Siddiqi (1961a, b), and Southwick, Ghosh, and Louch (1964) have reported on population surveys and social behavior of rhesus monkeys in cities and forested areas of North India. Lindberg (1967) and Neville (1966, 1968) have reported on the social behavior of rhesus monkeys inhabiting a forested area.

In order to judge the social behavior of rhesus monkeys living in artificial colonies, field studies are necessary to provide a standard of comparison. Cayo Santiago, Puerto Rico, the location of this study, is an island colony of rhesus monkeys descended from stock released there by C. R. Carpenter in 1938. Cayo Santiago was originally founded as a breeding colony and an area where unconfined monkeys could be observed from close at hand. Many important studies of this population have been made.

Carpenter observed the monkeys at Cayo Santiago for a six-week period in 1940, and he reported on their social organization and reproductive behavior (1942). Apart from this brief study, no information on the colony was available until the arrival of Altmann (1962), who studied the colony from June 1956 until May 1958. Carl B. Koford was in charge of the colony from 1958 to 1965, and during this period extensive observations concerned with social behavior and population were made by a number of investigators. In 1962, another rhesus monkey colony was founded in Puerto Rico near the village of La Parguera. The many publications resulting from observations at both Cayo Santiago and La Parguera are cited throughout this dissertation.

C. The Facilities at Cayo Santiago

Cayo Santiago is a 40-acre Caribbean island lying about five-eighths of a mile off the coast of Puerto Rico. It is located at latitude 18° 09' N. and longitude 65° 44' W. The island consists of two cays joined by an isthmus. The Big Cay rises 36 meters above sea level and the Small Cay is 22 meters high. Deciduous forest covers most of the Small Cay and the southern two-thirds of the Big Cay. The northern third of the Big Cay contains a mangrove swamp and a coconut palm plantation (Figures 1 and 2).

During my period of study there were seven feeders on the island, only six of which were operational, as feeder 1 had fallen into disrepair (see Figure 3). Feeders 1, 3, and 4 were located inside trapping cages. Blinds were located near the trapping cages, and the doors to the cages were left open unless monkeys were being trapped. Feeders 1, 2, 3, 5, 6, and 7 were situated on the Big Cay and feeder 4 on the Small Cay.

Two catchment basins were built to collect water during the rainy season. However, during the dry season, which extends from July to April (Koford 1965), the cisterns sometimes ran dry and water had to be brought from the mainland. Water is piped to all operational feeders.

Holding cages, a shop and toolshed, a pier and breakwater, and an unused building formerly functioning as a laboratory are also present on the island. On the mainland at the village of Playa de Humacao a compound containing two buildings, one with a shop and office and the other with an office only, provides air-conditioned work space for researchers at Cayo Santiago. A dock on the mainland and several motor launches facilitate travel to and from Cayo Santiago.

D. Materials, Methods, and Aims

Over 1400 hours of observations were made during an overall period from July 1965 to September 1967. A brief study of 2 months was made

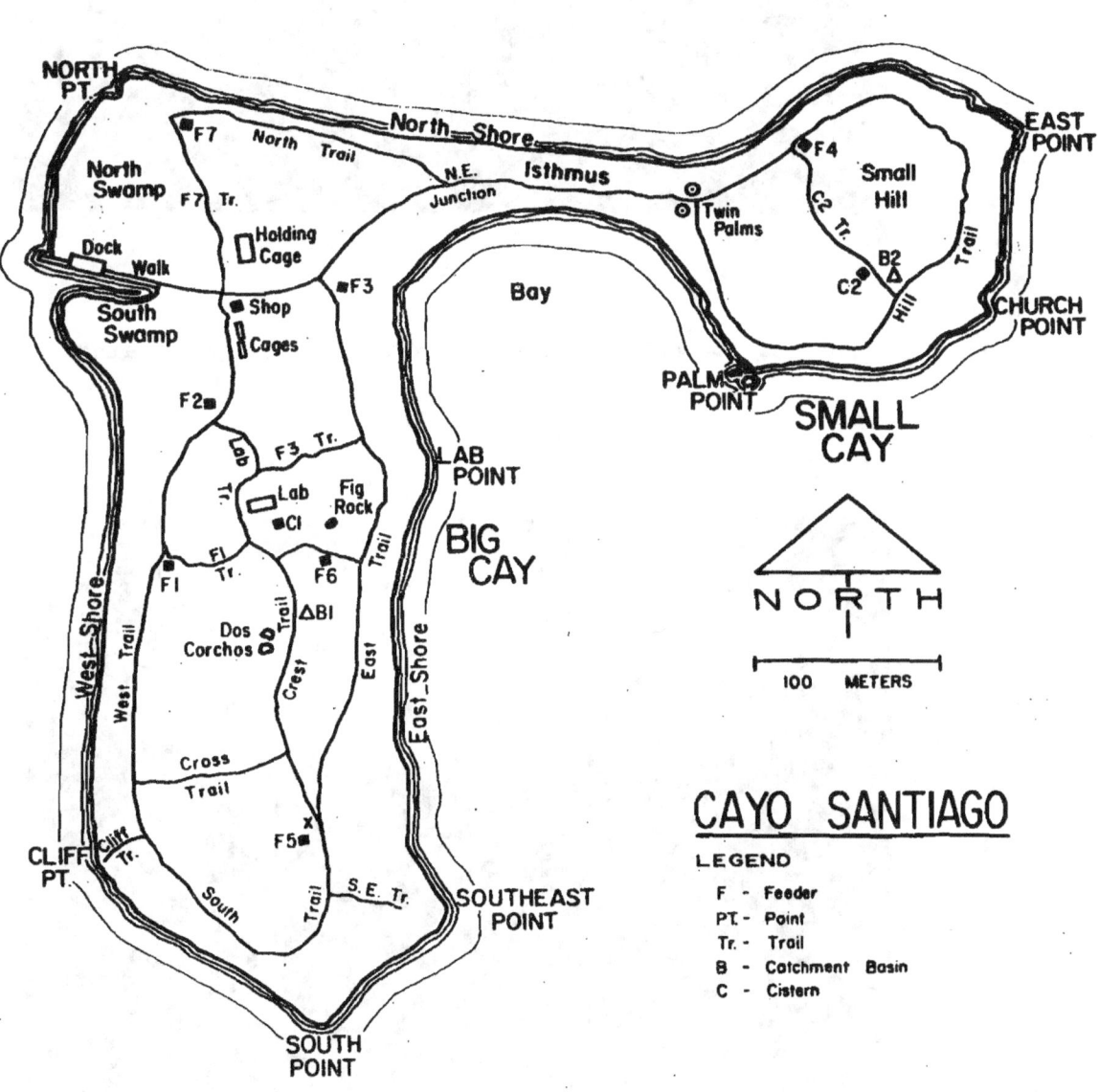

Figure 1. Map of Cayo Santiago

Cayo Santiago Island from El Yunque Mountain

Cayo Santiago Island from Mainland

Figure 2

Figure 3. Photographs of feeders and traps.

between July and September 1965, and a 12-month study was made between September 1966 and September 1967.

Field notes were supplemented by tape recordings of vocalizations, 8 mm movies and 35 mm still photographs; binoculars were used for observations. Altmann (1962) and Sade (1966) described the intricacies of habituating the monkeys to the observer, and other problems involved in observing at Cayo Santiago.

Almost all monkeys above the age of two years are tattooed, usually on the chest, face, or medial thigh. Since these marks are not always visible, however, positive identification of monkeys is not always possible, particularly during rapidly occurring agonistic behavior. Identification of monkeys under the age of three years is difficult because of their small size and high rate of activity. In general, it is easier to observe affectional behavior, such as grooming and tolerance of close spatial proximity, that occurs over a relatively long period of time, than it is to observe agonistic encounters which are usually less than several seconds in duration. Thus, slow motion film is particularly useful in analyzing agonistic behavior.

The aims of this study not only were to investigate agonistic behavior, but also to stress aspects of behavior at Cayo Santiago that have not been previously focused upon by other long-term studies. I thus singled out intergroup relations and nocturnal behavior as areas needing further investigation. As part of an attempt to relate gonadal hormones and reproductive behavior to aggression, I chose for particular attention five castrated male monkeys and one ovariectomized female in the colony; observations of male castrates were reported separately (Wilson and Vessey, in press). Seasonal variations in mortality and frequencies of wounding were studied as an indirect index of aggressive behavior.

E. Group Composition

Carpenter (1942) released 409 rhesus monkeys at Cayo Santiago in late 1938, and when he made a six-week study at the colony in 1940 he found that 350 monkeys were living in five social groups ranging in size from 147 to 13 individuals. An undetermined number of monkeys were removed from Cayo Santiago for use in medical research during World War II. When Stuart Altmann arrived at Cayo Santiago in 1956 he found only two social groups present, which he called Group 1 (later renamed Group B) and Group 2 (later renamed Group A). He completed a census in 1957 and found there were about 100 monkeys in Group B and about 55 in Group A.

In the fall of 1958 the monkeys of Group B split into two groups which were named Group C and Group D (Koford 1963a). In the fall of 1959, Koford observed that Group D had split into three factions which he named Groups G, E, and F. In the fall of 1960, Group G divided into two parts which were called Groups H and I. These groupings persisted for four years. In the fall of 1964 a group split off from Group A and was called Group J. As of September 1967 (the termination date of this study) the seven groups had not further divided (see Figure 4). Koford (1966) noted that 84 monkeys, mostly young males, were removed from the colony between 1959 and 1964, and that the population had grown about 16% per year during this period. The population changes and group composition during my period of study are seen in Tables 24, 25,

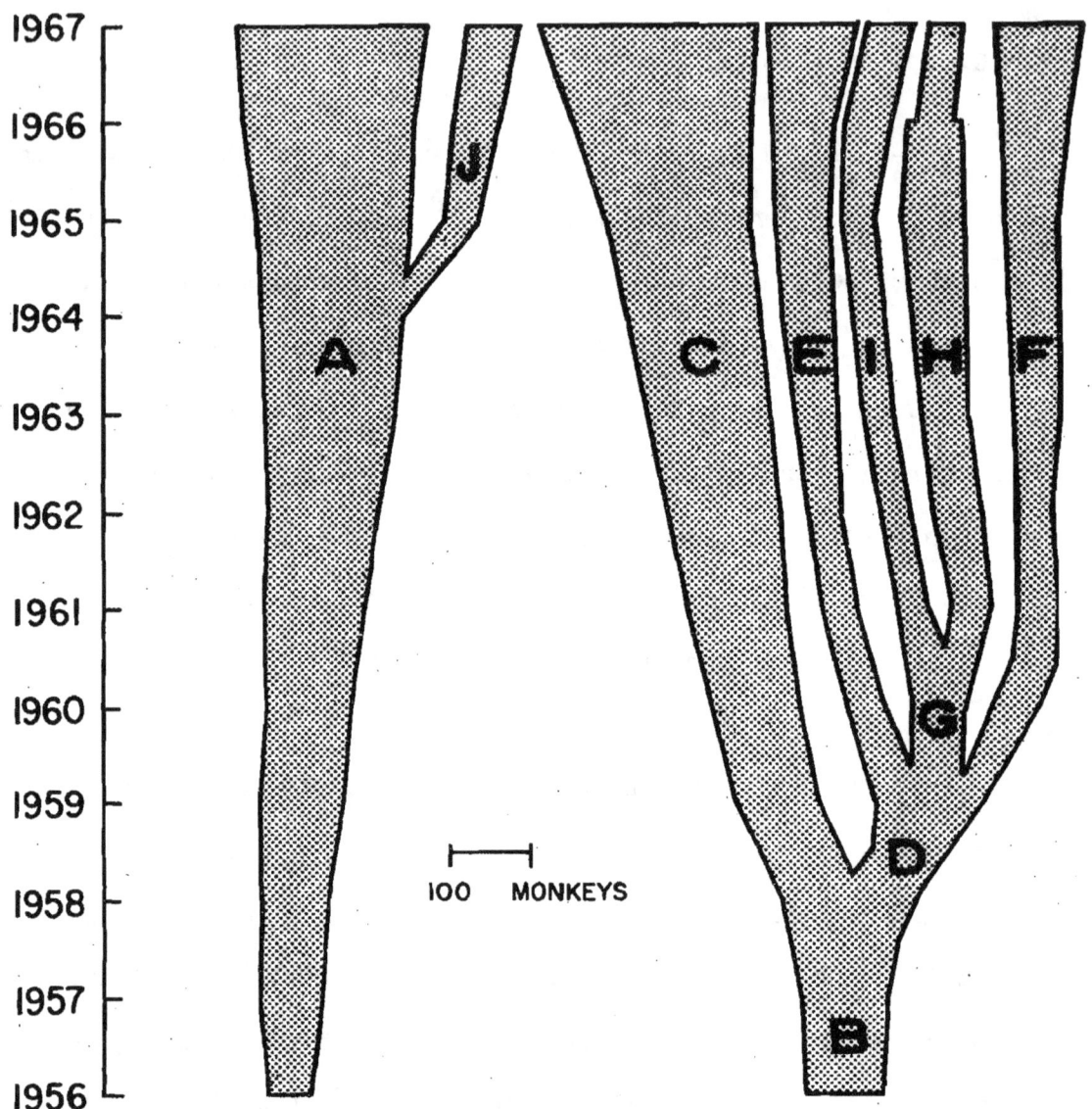

Figure 4. Population changes since 1956.
(modified after Koford 1963a)

Diagram illustrating growth and development from two groups in 1956
to seven groups in 1967. Vertical scale indicates time in years;
horizontal scale, numbers of monkeys. Large letters identify groups.

26, and 27 in the appendix. These tables may be referred to for detailed genealogical information, age, and group membership of individual monkeys whose social behavior is described in the following chapters.

F. Dispersion of Groups

Carpenter (1942) stated that in 1940 the five social groups at Cayo Santiago had distinct territories. This situation changed, however, in the following years. Altmann (1962) reported that all monkeys from both groups ranged over the entire island during his period of study. However, Group B rarely ventured onto the Small Cay while Group A was usually found either on the Small Cay or on the eastern side of the Big Cay. Altmann (1962) found in 1956 and Koford (1963a) found in 1963 that while Group A was the primary occupant of the Small Cay it was also observed in the eastern part of the Big Cay. When I arrived at Cayo Santiago in 1965 this situation still prevailed. Kaufmann (1967) reported that Group A had a peripheral male subgroup which tended to move closer to the main group during the breeding season. This was still the case through the fall of 1967. The peripheral male subgroup was also often spatially distinct from the rest of the group. Sometimes, the main portion of the main group was on the Small Cay, while the male subgroup was on the southern portion of the Big Cay.

Often, during the mating season (July to January) a peripheral male subgroup would remain on the Small Cay when the rest of the group would go on to the Big Cay. During the 1966 birth season, up to 40 males in the all-male subgroup ranging in age from two years to over ten years were counted. Kaufmann (1967) reported a subgroup composed of four-year-old males which constantly associated, but I saw no indication of such subgroups of like-aged males. Also, sometimes a male subgroup would travel with a female auxiliary composed of several adult females followed by immature offspring. The male subgroups will be described in more detail in Chapter IV.

Group A did not always travel as a distinct large group, although it frequently did at two times of the day. Just after dawn on mornings when Group A spent the night on the Big Cay, the group would come down out of the trees and run together in a column of about 50 monkeys, five abreast, each monkey being a distance of one or two meters from another. The group would quickly run from the hill of the Big Cay down along the eastern shore of the Big Cay and isthmus to the Small Cay. Sometimes at night, if Group A was on the Small Cay at dark it would run up to the sleeping area on the Big Cay, following the same route and mode of progression as it did on the morning trek.

Group A was sometimes dispersed over an area covering feeder 3, feeder 7, the isthmus, and the Small Cay. Often males and females of a subgroup, ranging in size upward from as few as ten individuals, would feed alone at feeder 3 or feeder 4 while the rest of the group occupied the Small Cay.

Since 1965, Group C (John A. Morrison, personal communication) has had a peculiar dispersion pattern unlike that for any other group on Cayo Santiago. It never travels together as a group, but instead is permanently divided into subgroups consisting of about 30 to 40 males and females of all ages. These appear as spatially distinct subgroups which travel together for periods of time ranging from one day to several weeks. However, both male and female membership in these sub-groups is constantly changing. While related females and their imma-ture offspring switch subgroups as family units, some males also associate together in their changes from subgroup to subgroup. Peripheral male subgroups with varying membership (up to 12 males observed in Group C subgroups) like the Group A male subgroups are also found in Group C.

Groups E, F, H, I, and J usually confine their wanderings to the Small Cay. Neither these groups nor any of the other groups at Cayo Santiago have peripheral male subgroups like those of Groups A and C.

G. Diurnal Activity Patterns

Diurnal activity patterns were strongly influenced by the work schedule of the staff which maintains the colony. While there were variations, the typical observation day at Cayo Santiago began at 0710 hours when the motor launch arrived at the island. On Monday, Wednesday, and Friday mornings, the monkeys were fed as soon as the boat docked. The caretakers, usually two or three men hired in Playa de Humacao, carried Purina Monkey Chow to the feeders. On some days, the diet was supplemented with bananas, plantains, and cattle chow. The monkeys also browsed on vegetation and sometimes ate insects. Mr. Angel Figueroa, chief caretaker, attempted to census the entire population each month. His observations were usually conducted in the morning.

Monkeys usually waited for the boat at the pier, particularly on feeding days. This welcoming committee was typically made up of Group C members. A high-ranking male sometimes jumped up and down on the roof of the shelter covering the pier as the boat came in, and the island began to resound with clear calls (Rowell and Hinde 1962) as other monkeys took up the cry. Adult females and immatures were the most vocal. When the boat was unloaded, monkeys scampered about the pier. If a bag broke, pellets were grabbed and fights broke out in the excitement. The caretakers carrying sacks of chow to the feeders were followed by monkeys.

After the feeders were filled, monkeys of all ages and sexes rushed in to feed. High-ranking monkeys supplanted low-ranking individuals at the feeders, although they were not invariably the first to feed. Some low-ranking monkeys were tolerated while feeding next to high-ranking monkeys, depending, perhaps, on the affectional ties between them and the personality and mood of the dominant animal.

Group C was the first to feed at feeder 2 on feeding days and Group A was first at feeder 4. The first to feed at feeder 3 was usually either Group C or Group A. Feeders 5, 6, and 7 were more variable as to which group occupied them first. Group A frequently occupied feeder 4 for the entire morning. Often, however, this group fed there for less than an hour before all or part of the group wandered over the isthmus to visit the feeders on the Big Cay.

The groups moved from feeder to feeder throughout most of the morning. While small groups usually gave way at feeders to larger groups (see Chapter IV), the two largest groups, A and C, voluntarily moved away from feeders that were still full of chow to visit other feeders. I have observed monkeys in Groups A and C visit up to five feeders between 0730 and 1000 hours. The other groups also engaged in these peripatetic feeding habits, often being supplanted at one feeder by a larger group. Groups stayed at each feeder, generally, from 15 minutes to an hour, although the time each individual spent at each feeder was highly variable. Group C, which was always broken up into spatially distinct subgroups, and Group A, which often was divided in such a manner, sometimes occupied several feeders simultaneously.

While some group members took their turn at the feeders, other monkeys fought, groomed, played, copulated, or rested nearby. After high-ranking monkeys in a group had eaten, they left the vicinity of the feeder, while low-ranking members of the same group remained. Such low-ranking stragglers from high-ranking groups were sometimes driven from the feeder by low-ranking groups.

A lower rate of group interaction and a general decrease in individual movements accompanied the rise of temperature and the overhead sun after 1030 hours. Human observers were affected by the same sluggishness shown by the monkeys. The afternoon was a period when groups spent several hours in one spot away from the feeders, engaging in social activities or resting. As the sun dropped in the sky, the rate of group movement began to increase and the monkeys became more active. By 1700 hours the groups were again moving from feeder to feeder as they did in the morning.

II. NOCTURNAL BEHAVIOR

A. Introduction

Washburn and Hamburg (1965a,b) pointed out that most studies of free-ranging nonhuman primates have dealt largely with observations made during daylight hours. As they point out, however, nocturnal behaviors are extremely important as adaptations from an evolutionary perspective, and are thus worthy of more extensive field work. In this chapter, observations of the nocturnal behavior of rhesus monkeys at Cayo Santiago will be presented and then compared with what is known about the nocturnal behavior of free-ranging Old World monkeys and apes.

B. Methods

From November 1966 to September 1967 I spent a total of 36 nights on Cayo Santiago. At least one night during each of these months was spent on the island. Thirty nights of observations were made during the nonmating season and six during the mating season.

For long-term observations on monkeys in the trees it was convenient to use an aluminum lawn chair that was either placed near locations favored by the monkeys for sleeping or brought to the area after they had roosted. Several hours before sunset I wore sunglasses to accustom my eyes to the dark. I used 8×40 mm binoculars for the observations, and took field notes with the aid of a penlight-flashlight. A regular flashlight proved unsatisfactory for purposes of observation because the monkeys became disturbed and ran away when it was pointed at them;

thus I used mine very sparingly. On moonlit nights, light from the
stars and moon was usually sufficient for moving about and discerning
silhouettes of monkeys in the trees.

During these observations I made tape recordings of vocalizations
heard in the areas of study.

C. Dispersion of Groups at Night

Monkeys in all groups usually slept on the leeward side of the
Big Cay hill because a breeze from the northeast often blew throughout
the night, and the monkeys preferred to stay out of the wind. On
eight out of 36 nights, Group A, the group which has almost exclusive
use of the Small Cay, slept on the leeward side of the Small Cay.
Group J, the small group which split off from Group A in 1964, spent
five nights on the Small Cay and on two of those nights, Groups J and
A were both sleeping on the Small Cay. No other groups were observed
sleeping on the Small Cay. Monkeys were seen sleeping in the mangroves
on three nights and in the coconut palms on four nights; however,
their groups were not identified. On two nights, an estimated four to
seven peripheral males of Group A spent the night on the Small Cay
while the rest of the group slept on the Big Cay. Sleeping areas are
shown in Figure 5.

Because monkeys continued to shift positions until after dark, it
was rarely possible to determine spatially distinct sleeping locations
for each group within the Big Cay. On two nights, Group I was seen to
roost by itself in trees on the southern tip of the island. Group C
monkeys were observed to sleep on the west side of the Big Cay, but
the group boundaries were not observed. Whether or not Group C

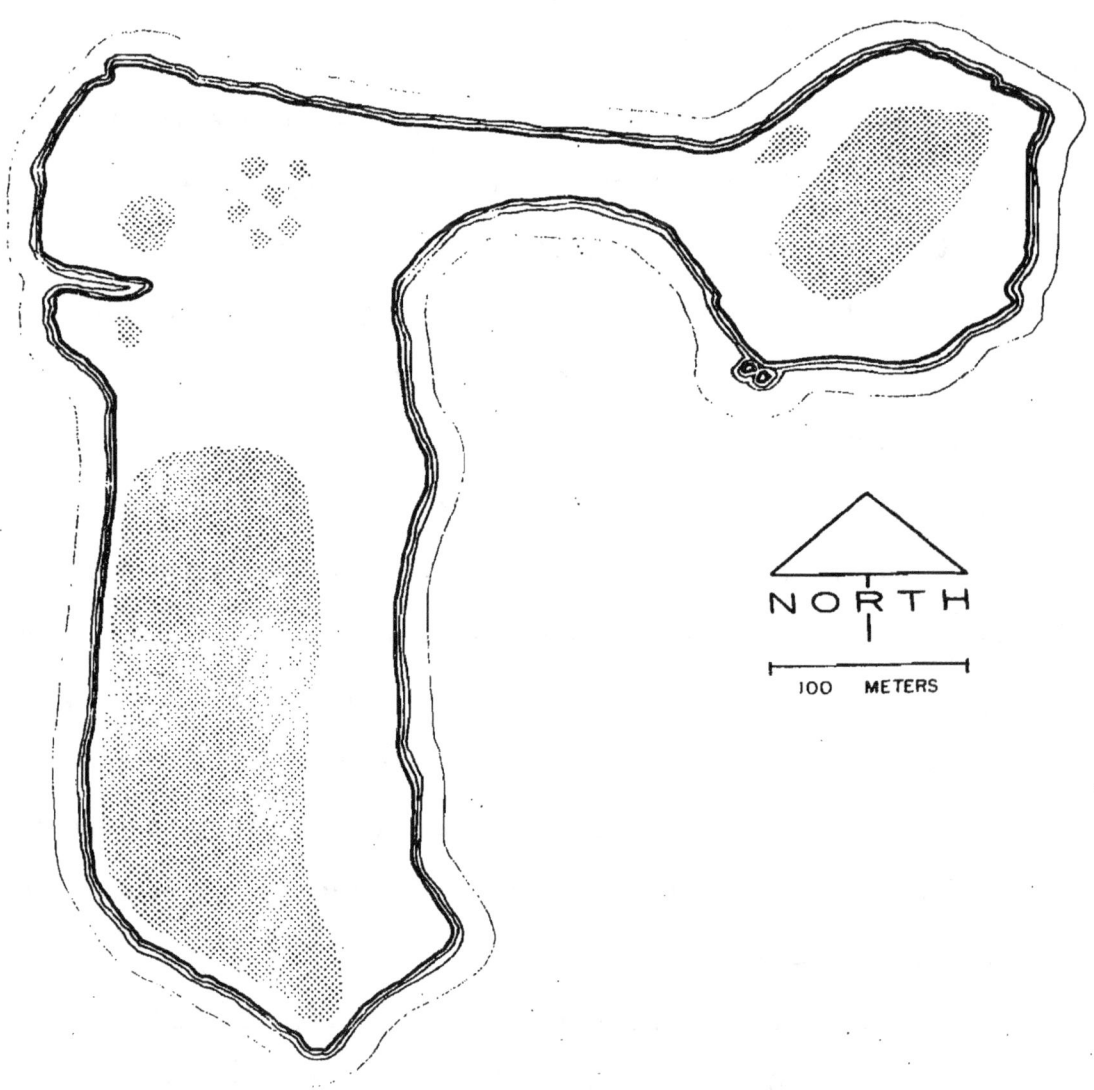

Figure 5.   Sleeping areas.

Shaded areas show where monkeys were observed sleeping.

retained its diurnal permanent subgroupings at night was not determined. Most of the night all monkeys slept in trees that were from five to over fifteen meters above the ground. The dense foliage in the sleeping area was not conducive to fixing group boundaries. Roosting areas in the mangrove swamp and palm trees were difficult to locate because the monkeys usually shifted positions until after dark. Attempts to use a flashlight were unsatisfactory, as previously explained.

When Groups A and J slept on the Small Cay, however, definite group boundaries were seen. Group J monkeys that were settled for the night stayed within an area approximately 20 meters in diameter and roosted in from three to six trees. Group A monkeys sleeping on the Small Cay occupied an area approximately 100 meters long and 75 meters wide.

D. Progression of Groups to Sleeping Areas

Typically, one to two hours before sunset, the groups began moving toward the hill of the Big Cay. Group A was usually the last to arrive. On four days Group J waited near the isthmus on the Big Cay for Group A to leave the Small Cay and then followed it up to the hill of the Big Cay. On nights that Group A slept on the Big Cay hill it visited the feeder on the Small Cay before beginning its progression to the sleeping area. Group A invariably went to the Big Cay hill sleeping area along the east shore while Group C usually went by way of the west shore. The five smaller groups most often traveled up the middle portion of the island, generally arriving at the sleeping area before Groups A and C. On the way to the sleeping areas monkeys briefly fed at the feeders. Although dominant males of each group were frequently seen leading their groups to roosting places during this period, such direction of group movements by the dominant male was rarely observed during the day. [For a description of group progression during the day, see Kaufmann (1967) and Sade (1966).] At dusk, the monkeys were less tolerant of the presence of a human observer, and high-ranking males usually stayed near me while I was following a group.

E. Increased Agonistic Behavior at Dusk

Fights were more frequent at dusk than at any other period of the day, particularly during the mating season. This was unfortunate, considering my interest in identifying individuals involved in agonistic interactions. In the mating season, vocalizations associated with severe fighting (Rowell 1962) were often continuous on the Big Cay from half an hour before sunset to an hour after sunset when most or all groups were concentrated on the west slope of the hill which was slightly larger than 200 by 100 meters in area. Tape recordings made during this period with the aid of a parabolic reflector contain sequences where agonistic vocalizations are heard continuously throughout the half-hour tape. During this period some adult males ran through the various groups seemingly at random. When these males came across another similarly excited male, a fight ensued. Such excited intergroup combat was observed and heard only on eight evenings, on the crest of the Big Cay hill between feeder 5 and catchment basin 1 (see Figure 1). Intergroup fighting was observed to have occurred outside of the mating season on two evenings, one in January and one in March. One incident of severe intergroup fighting and several intergroup copulations occurred on December 5, 1966, and is described in detail in Chapter IV. In contrast to intergroup fights which took place during the day, coalitions between group members were not observed at dusk, when often two males from the same group would engage in combat.

F. Effects of Moonlight on Nocturnal Activity

On nights with bright moonlight, monkeys would sometimes display behavior usually associated with diurnal activities, such as feeding, copulating, and agonistic play. However, on four nights with a full moon no ground activity was observed. Nocturnal ground activity was never observed on nights with less than half a moon.

A typical consort relationship between a male and a female was seen in the light of the full moon at 2200 hours, 22 August 1967, with four mounts consisting of five to 40 pelvic thrusts interspersed by grooming bouts approximately 3 minutes in duration. Then the male, followed by the female, ran off on the ground. Throughout this night some monkeys fed at the feeders, fought, and walked about the ground, while others slept. On eight nights which were lit by a full to a half moon, monkeys were seen wandering about the ground (more than five monkeys were seen on each night for at least 6 hours after dark). All cases of nocturnal ground activity were seen in the Big Cay hill sleeping area, primarily on the crest of the Big Cay hill between feeder 5 and catchment basin 1. Even on nights with a full moon many monkeys either moved about in the trees or stayed in sleeping positions. On nights when many monkeys came to the ground it was not possible to estimate the proportion of monkeys in trees to those on the ground.

G. Sleeping Positions, Ascent and Descent from the Trees

It was noted that monkeys did not confine their sleeping to the night as some were observed sleeping during the day, particularly during the midday heat. During the day the monkeys slept in a variety of positions, either on their backs, sides, or ischial callosities, in trees or on the ground. Chester Swett (personal communication) has been studying the sleep behavior of the monkey during the day, and a good estimate of the amount of time they spend in diurnal sleeping should soon be available. Mothers and infants usually slept on their sides facing each other, and adult monkeys sleeping in pairs assumed the same position. Often one monkey in the pair placed its head in the lap of its partner and wrapped its arms around its partner's waist, while the partner leaned over and wrapped its arms over the first monkey, as both assumed a sitting position making a compact ball of fur, thus exposing a minimum of surface area to the elements. Individual monkeys often slept in crotches of trees, resting their feet on one branch and their ischial callosities on the other, and laying their heads on their thighs while wrapping their arms about their knees.

Monkeys slept at night almost exclusively off the ground. Starting about half an hour before sunset they began to settle into the trees. The periods of time they rested in one place, however, were highly variable, and some shifting took place throughout the night. Usually, as the evening progressed the amount of shifting of positions decreased. The relative amount of shifting was noted by watching silhouettes and hearing the movements of monkeys in the foliage.

From about half an hour before sunset to as long as an hour after sunset a chorus of clear calls (Rowell and Hinde 1962) was heard. These were made primarily by monkeys under four years of age and by adult females. Rowell and Hinde (1962), in their studies of rhesus monkey vocalization, found that they could differentiate individual monkeys by their clear calls. At Cayo Santiago, a clear call by one monkey was often followed by an answering call by another monkey at a different pitch. Whether or not monkeys could recognize individuals or groups by their clear calls was not determined.

Because shifting of position continued until well after dark, identification of individuals making up huddle groups was usually impossible. However, from observations of sleeping huddle groups seen during the day and from less accurate nocturnal observations the following tentative generalizations concerning the composition of sleeping huddle groups seems in order. Huddle groups of two and monkeys sleeping alone were the most frequent combination. Huddle groups were largest on cool nights when as many as six monkeys were observed sleeping on one strong branch. Mother-infant, mother-daughter, brother-brother, and other combinations of relatives were common sleeping pairs. During the mating season, two different consort pairs along with the female's infant were observed to sleep together. Although adult males often slept alone, three pairs who were seen associating with each other frequently during the day were seen sleeping together at night on one occasion each. Steven Vessey (personal communication), using an infrared sniperscope, is studying the composition of sleeping subgroups of rhesus monkeys at the La Parguera colony, and we will soon have much more detailed information concerning this question.

Mothers with infants were usually the first to get into their places, and they shifted less than other monkeys, whereas monkeys from one to four years old were the most active and often chased each other before settling down for the night. Some adult males and females rested on the ground for over half an hour after sunset before climbing into the trees. High-ranking males were usually the last to leave the ground.

In the morning, generally about half an hour before sunrise, young monkeys between the ages of one and four years began to scamper about in the trees and increasing numbers of clear calls were heard. Older monkeys began to move around gradually about ten minutes after the younger ones. On the two rainy, cloudy mornings that observations were made, monkeys did not leave their sleeping positions until several hours after sunrise, when the rain had diminished.

High-ranking males came to the ground first. When Group A spent the night on the Big Cay, it ran back to the Small Cay along the east shore immediately after descending from the trees, while Group C fanned out over the west shore and the other groups spread out over the rest of the island. By half an hour after sunrise, the groups were dispersed over the island.

H. Discussion

Because Cayo Santiago is an artificial colony and not the native habitat of the rhesus monkey, it may be useful to compare the nocturnal behavior of this Old World species transplanted to a small Caribbean island with what is known concerning the nocturnal behavior of other free-ranging nonhuman primates in their native habitats. Washburn and Hamburg (1965a,b) have pointed out several generalizations concerning the nocturnal and sleeping behavior of free-ranging nonhuman primates: (1) All monkeys and apes sleep in groups, usually in trees. (2) A major reason that some monkeys and apes may become ground-living is that their pattern of activity keeps them away from the normal hunting of lions, leopards, and many other predators. (3) Monkeys have evolved specialized sitting pads, ischial callosities, that permit them to sleep sitting upright in the trees in comfort. (4) The distribution of suitable sleeping trees may limit the distribution of nonhuman primates, with two important exceptions: gorillas, which are so large that they sleep on the ground (Schaller 1965), and baboons, which may sleep on rock ledges or cliffs providing limited access to predators (Kummer and Kurt 1963). (5) Learning is also found to be extremely important in primate sleeping habits. Primates may learn which areas are suitable for sleeping; the construction of sleeping nests by chimpanzees (Goodall 1965, Reynolds and Reynolds 1965) is also thought to be at least partially learned (Bernstein 1962).

It was noted that fighting at Cayo Santiago was most frequent at dusk before the monkeys roosted for the night. Struhsaker (1967a) reported a similar increase in agonistic behavior at dusk among Cercopithecus aethiops in Kenya. In Senegal, Bert, Ayats, Martino, and Collomb (1967) observed a high level of chasing among Papio papio juveniles in trees at dusk before they settled into sleeping positions. According to Southwick et al. (1965), rhesus monkeys living near a temple in North India were characterized by increased intragroup aggressiveness during the last hour before darkness. Struhsaker (1967a) suggests that an increase in agonistic encounters at dusk may enhance the formation of sleeping subgroups, and this temporary separation of group members into sleeping subgroups may eventually lead to a gradual formation of new and separate social groups. He theorizes that such a gradual parting would have advantages over a more rapid one. It would allow the population to expand and explore new regions while maintaining a familiar area as a food source and refuge from predators. Struhsaker also reviewed published reports on the sizes of sleeping subgroups in species of African monkeys, and he remarked on the extraordinary similarity in the size of sleeping subgroups among the five species (see Table 1). Sleeping subgroups of temple monkeys reported by Southwick et al. were larger than those observed at Cayo Santiago. It may be that larger sleeping subgroups were possible in the temple rhesus monkeys because they often slept on flat rooftops where room was available for large subgroups to form. The size of sleeping subgroups at Cayo Santiago was limited by the number of monkeys each roosting place in the trees would support. Although Bert et al. (1967) did not estimate the size of sleeping subgroups, their paper included a photograph taken of Papio papio in trees at night in which no subgroup larger than three monkeys was noted. Struhsaker (1967a) reported that mother-infant, mother-yearling, and coalitionary relations often slept together as subgroups among Ceropithecus aethiops; as mentioned previously, these sleeping arrangements were also evident among the Macaca mulatta at Cayo Santiago.

Southwick et al. (1965) stated that group movement of the Indian temple monkeys began half an hour before dawn and that after about 15 minutes each group generally moved out from the sleeping areas in a stereotyped characteristic path. This behavior is similar to that of the Cayo Santiago monkeys at dawn.

Reports of Lumsden (1951), Bert et al. (1967), Southwick et al. (1965), and Struhsaker (1967b), as well as data obtained at Cayo Santiago,

TABLE 1

COMPARISON OF SLEEPING SUBGROUP SIZE

(After Struhsaker 1967a)

Species	Author	Size of Sleeping Subgroups				
		Range	Mode	Mean (including solitaries)	Mean (excluding solitaries)
Cercopithecus aethiops	Struhsaker (1967)	1-14	1 and 3	4.22	4.65
Cercopithecus ascanius	Buxton (1952)	-	-	-	3.64
Cercopithecus ascanius	Lumsden (1951)	2-12	4	4.81	4.81
Cercopithecus mitis	Lumsden (1951)	1-8	4	3.53	3.92
Papio doguera	Lumsden (1951)	1-10	4	4.43	4.66
Cercocebus albigena	Lumsden (1951)	1-13	4	4.35	4.42
Macaca mulatta	Southwick et al. (1965)	2-15	-	-	-
Macaca mulatta	Wilson (this paper)	1-6	2	2.36	-

all indicate that while certain sleeping areas are preferred, there is no reliance on a single nocturnal refuge among a wide range of Old World monkeys. Bert et al. reported, however, that Papio papio, in the area they studied, remained in the same sleeping positions throughout the night. This was unlike rhesus monkeys at Cayo Santiago which were observed to shift positions at night, particularly in bright moonlight. Neville (1968) noted that rhesus monkeys in towns may stay awake at night in lighted areas.

While the relative amount of movement at night among free-ranging nonhuman primates is unknown, it is known that all mammals have recurring periods of greater responsiveness to sensory stimuli following dreaming or rapid eye movement (REM) sleep (Roffwarg, Musio, and Dement 1966). Snyder (1966) has proposed several possible survival functions of REM sleep in mammals in his paper "Toward an Evolutionary Theory of Dreaming": (1) Muscular twitching in the REM state may aid in temperature regulation during sustained sleep. (2) A sentinel or vigilance function is proposed in which the periodic awakenings which follow the REM period are used to sample the environment for danger. (3) The muscular and nervous activity of the REM period may provide preparatory activation prior to each sentinel awakening, so that if flight is needed the animal is prepared for it.

Whatever the adaptive value of sleep and dreaming turns out to be in terms of the evolution of the nonhuman primates, the meanings of dreams for man require more detailed research. Perhaps studies of sleep in the nonhuman primates may someday help man to understand the origins and adaptive value of his own nocturnal behavior patterns.

III. SEASONAL FLUCTUATIONS IN AGGRESSION AND SOCIAL DOMINANCE AND
THEIR RELATIONSHIP TO REPRODUCTIVE BEHAVIOR

A. Introduction

In 1940, at Cayo Santiago (Carpenter 1942), the marked seasonal
variations in reproductive behavior which Altmann (1962) found there in
1956 had not yet become fixed. Since 1956, however, detailed studies
of reproductive behavior at the colony have established that definite
mating and birth seasons do now exist. Copulations leading to concep-
tion occur only between the months of July and January, and births
occur only between January and July (Kaufmann 1965, Koford 1965,
Conaway and Koford 1965).

Kaufmann (1967) reported that agonistic social interactions of
Group A males increased during the mating period and were greatest
during the transition period between nonmating and mating seasons.
Sade (1966:36) found "within Group F that general aggressiveness, as
indicated by the number of fights between all classes of monkeys, was
greatest in the transition period between the birth and mating season,
and that it gradually lessened to about half its peak as the nonmating
season approached." This chapter will point out that mortality, wound
frequencies, and changes in dominance status are also seasonal at Cayo
Santiago and that such seasonal variations in aggressive behavior may
be related to reproduction.

B. Methods Used in Determining Dominance Status

Before outlining the criteria that were used in this study for
dominance relations of free-ranging rhesus monkeys, the criteria used

in earlier studies should be reviewed. While the criteria of dominance used by investigators working with caged rhesus monkeys are extensive (Mason 1961, Maslow 1935), the problems involved in ascertaining dominance relations in caged animals are different from those in the field and a discussion of those criteria is beyond the scope of this section. One monkey is said to be dominant to another if the other monkey gives way to it in competition over food, space, or estrus females.

Altmann (1962) stated that the dominance status of rhesus monkeys was communicated by a number of behavior patterns. Dominant monkeys communicated their status by: (1) a brisk striding gait, (2) calm sitting posture, (3) standing with tail erect, (4) mounting of other individuals, and (5) "perhaps by watching other individuals." Subordination was indicated by: (1) testis retraction, (2) grimacing, (3) avoiding staring, and (4) sexual presenting. In addition to these "universal" status indicators, monkeys apparently recognized each other as individuals and acted accordingly.

Southwick et al. (1965) based their criteria of dominance on the outcome of "aggressive encounters." They did not break down the term aggressive encounter into smaller units of analysis and include both natural encounters and forced encounters where food was placed equidistant between two monkeys.

Koford (1963a) judged dominance on the basis of observations of the exchange of threatening and submissive gestures and by precedence at food and water. Threatening gestures noted by Koford (1963b) were: (1) approaching, (2) staring, (3) brow raising, (4) lowering the forebody, (5) bobbing the head, (6) poking the muzzle forward, (7) huffing repeatedly (pant-threat), (8) feinting attacks, and (9) rushing forward in "snarling charges." Submissive gestures were: (1) casual disregard, (2) looking away, (3) walking away, (4) working the protruded lips (lip-smacking), displaying the closed teeth in a grin (grimacing), (5) cringing, (6) presenting the anal region toward the aggressor, and (7) fleeing headlong. Observation of threat by one monkey followed by another's submissive response seemed to be a reliable indicator of social order.

Kaufmann (1967) defined dominance in rhesus males on the basis of "spatial displacements and the exchange of aggressive and submissive signals." Aggressive signals were classified as follows: (1) "Break up fights" (of other monkeys) was considered to be a special case of threatening. (2) "Attack" was any hostile encounter involving physical combat. (3) "Active displacement" involved an overt threat by which one monkey caused another to move aside. (4) "Passive displacement" involved no overt threat. (5) "Threat (without displacement)" involved staring or running toward another monkey "often with the mouth open and with a threat call." (6) Tree-shaking was considered a long distance threat directed at foreign objects or members of other bands. (7) Another special form of threat involved a high-ranking male walking very close to another monkey or even around it in a tight circle. At the same time he would thrust his face close to the other's face and protrude his lips. The threatened monkey responded by sitting very still and giving a fear grin. This ritual was never followed by attack. Having observed this behavior pattern, I considered it to be pacificatory because it brought about a cessation of intragroup fighting (see Appendix B). (8) A single brief mounting, with or without pelvic thrusts, was interpreted as an aggressive act. This type of mounting was distinguished from true copulation where repeated mountings of females culminated in ejaculation. Kaufmann noted that mounting between males was a poor indicator of dominance because in only 10 out of 39 mounting interactions was the dominant male the mounter. (9) "Appeased" was an "aggressive act" listed but not discussed.

Submissive displays were: (1) attacked, (2) displaced, active, (3) displaced, passive, (4) threatened (no displacement, (5) mounted, and (6) appeased.

Sade (1967) determined dominance rank on the basis of observations of "fights." A fight is defined as an interaction in which an attack is of any intensity. The components of attack are: (1) stare, (2) move toward, (3) bob, (4) stalk, (5) lunge, (6) charge, (7) push, (8) bat, (9) grab-release, (10) grab-hold, (11) open-mouth, (12) ears-brow-eyelids, (13) bite, (14) grunt, and (15) roar. The components of flight are: (1) glance away, (2) cower, (3) move aside, (4) hop aside, (5) present, (6) flee, (7) grimace, (8) hiss, (9) squeak, and (10) shriek. Sade noted that these terms represent points on a continuum rather than discrete units of behavior. Success in obtaining food was not used as a criteria for winning a fight. Although food was occasionally used to start fights between monkeys, the loser of a fight sometimes took the food. Mounting, lip-smacking, grooming, yawning, and tail position were specifically excluded as being predictive of dominance relationships.

Carpenter (1942), in his studies of the Cayo Santiago colony, gave a male dominance order based on "all observable variations in behavior and group status"; he judged dominance on the basis of "all behavior classified as having any degree of aggressiveness." However, he did not give a detailed description of the displays he used in ascertaining dominance.

Lindburg (1966: 87-88) determined dominance on the basis of
(1) feeding tests, (2) the outcome of aggressive encounters, (3) viewing
subordinate displays, and (4) spatial relationships. He stated that
although the results were the same when these criteria were used with
respect to males, females could only be considered high-ranking in terms
of high-dominant or low-dominant categories rather than in a linear
hierarchy.

Neville (1966: 192,213) gave no clear-cut listing of criteria for
dominance relationships. He feels that dominance hierarchies and agonistic behavior have been overemphasized in relation to their importance in
free-ranging situations. "One adult male is usually dominant over the
rest of the troop. This dominance is expressed by the caution shown by
the other monkeys in interactions with this male, the 'social space'
around the male and the assurance of the male. Male dominance hierarchies are relatively stable and potentially last years."

The criteria used by these fieldworkers were of great value to me
in setting up my own criteria for dominance. I tried to find agonistic
displays indicating dominance that were: (1) easily seen in the environment of Cayo Santiago under all conditions of observation, and (2) unam-
biguously predictive of dominance relationships.

After attempting to use the criteria established by the above-
mentioned authors for assessing dominance, I encountered certain problems.
First, not all agonistic displays in an interaction could be seen and
noted (both in field notes and on checklist sheets) with equal facility.
Second, different agonistic displays were not consistent with each
other as far as predicting dominance was concerned.

Grimacing and supplanting were the two most frequent categories of agonistic behavior noted, probably because they were the easiest to observe. Supplantations occurred frequently at the feeders and as the monkeys moved about on the ground. Since many supplantations took place while monkeys were moving about slowly, there was adequate time for positive identification of several monkeys in an interaction. In rapidly occurring agonistic interactions that may last only a few seconds and which may involve several monkeys, five or more components of agonistic display may occur simultaneously in the various partici- pants. It is impossible to note all of these and at the same time to identify the participants. This is particularly true as the distance increases between the observer and the monkeys involved. The flash of grimace was the agonistic display most easily observed over a distance.

Although both grimacing and supplanting were observed more fre- quently than other agonistic behaviors, they were not of equal predictive value in assigning dominance relationships. Supplanting interactions in which a subordinate monkey supplants a higher-ranking monkey occur fre- quently (see Appendix B). In contrast to supplanting, grimacing was almost never directed toward a monkey known to be the grimacing monkey's subordinate. Rare exceptions to this are noted in Appendix B. Agonistic displays other than grimacing were often found to be misleading in pre- dicting dominance. This is not to say, however, that grimacing was the only criteria used in judging dominance. I considered all observable agonistic behaviors in my criteria for dominance, but positive dominance relationships were determined only if I observed the subordinate monkey consistently grimacing toward its superior. Grimacing usually occurred along with other submissive behavior.

A variety of food, usually raisins, plantains, or apples, were used to elicit agonistic behavior from the monkeys. As Sade (1967) found, the dominant monkey did not always get the food; however, the agonistic interactions observed in the context of "food tests" were very useful in ascertaining dominance relationships. This was particularly true of monkeys that appeared to avoid each other within a group and usually maintained spatial distances of over 15 meters. In order to observe their agonistic interactions over food, I often attempted to lure monkeys together whose dominance relations were unknown. This was done by leading one monkey toward another with a trail of food. Many of the monkeys, however, refused to move close enough together for me to observe interactions between them, since their avoidance of each other could not be overcome with a food incentive.

C. Female Dominance

The dominance rank of females seems to be largely determined by the dominance rank of their female lines (Sade 1967). A female line includes a founding female and her descendants. Complete genealogies are not available because the females consort with several males during estrus, thus rendering impossible the identification of the sires of individual monkeys. All infants are tattooed and their mothers are noted so that genealogical information giving descent through females is available for monkeys born as early as 1956. Although females from low-ranking female lines do not become dominant to females belonging to high-ranking lines, on occasion, combat between them results in a low-ranking female winning an agonistic encounter. Such breaches of the female line dominance hierarchy are usually followed immediately by punishment of the transgressor by adult males of the group and members of the high-ranking female line. In no case was a consistent dominance reversal between females of different lines observed. However, Marsden (1968), working at the La Parguera rhesus monkey colony, reversed the dominance between two female lines by removing the founding female of the previously dominant line.

An example of the corporate nature of the ranked female line could be seen in Group J which had only two female lines. Out of 68 dominance interactions between females of these two lines, 54 resulted in the dominant female line member winning the dominance interaction even when she was younger and smaller in size than her opponent (see Table 2). When a female from a low-ranking female line attacked a member of a higher-ranking female line (usually in response to the low-ranking female's infant being threatened by a high-ranking female), the low-ranking female was invariably chased by the high-ranking female's relatives and/or by adult males in the group, whether or not they were related to the females involved in the encounter.

The dominance of females and their female lines is not due to the number of individuals in a line. While in Group J, the female line with the most members is dominant, this is not the case in other groups. Sade (in press) points out that the two highest ranking lines in Group F have fewer members than the four lower-ranking lines (see Table 3). Moreover, the relative dominance of one line over another has not changed over the years in any group on Cayo Santiago which Sade (1967) or I have studied.

Sade (1967) noted in two cases that females within each line tend to become dominant to their older sisters as they reach their first

TABLE 2

DOMINANCE INTERACTIONS BETWEEN FEMALES OF TWO FEMALE LINES IN GROUP J

All Females in Female Line 1 are Descended from Female 92

All Females in Female Line 2 are Descended from Female 31

Female Line 1*	Number of Times Female in Family 1 Dominated Female in Family 2
92	11
TN	12
S09	12
XQ	5
LA	14
K9	-
	54

Female Line 2†	Number of Times Female in Family 2 Dominated Female in Family 1
31	3
WF	1
XJ	1
JP	3
	8

* Female Line 1 members dominated Family 2 members an average of 9 times per individual.

† Female Line 2 members dominated Family 1 members an average of 2 times per individual.

TABLE 3

RELATIONSHIP OF NUMBER OF MONKEYS IN FEMALE LINE TO LINE DOMINANCE

Female Lines in Group F (from Sade, in press) in 1955 in
Order of Decreasing Dominance

1.	Line 1	(9 members, 4 females)
2.	Line 2	(6 members, 3 females)
3.	Line 3	(12 members, 3 females)
4.	Line 4	(14 members, 7 females)
5.	Line 5	(15 members, 7 females)
6.	Line 7	(12 members, 6 females)

estrus. I observed dominance interactions between six pairs of sisters all of which had had at least one estrus, and in four of these pairs, the younger sister was dominant. In four pairs of sisters where the older one had had at least one estrus but the younger one had not, the older sister was invariably dominant (see Table 4). Thus all observed female dominance changes occurred at the onset of the mating season.

Females in consort with a male are usually dominant to males which are subordinate to their consort. These dominance interactions are not considered in setting up dominance hierarchies since they are cases of derived dominance, such as that which an infant enjoys while in the company of its mother when she is dominant to the monkeys with which the infant is interacting.

Young females derive their dominance status largely from the status of their mothers, who support them in their initial encounters with females from other female lines. Such coalitions are noted in Table 12. No triangular dominance relationships between females were noted. (A triangular dominance relationship is one in which A dominates B, B dominates C, and C dominates A.) Thus female lines form subgroups which are ranked in dominance within the larger group.

D. Male Dominance

Dominance relationships of males, unlike those of females, are not relatively stable and predictable over the years. While it is true that some males from high-ranking female lines tend to rise to high dominance positions in their natal groups at a younger age than males from low-ranking lines (Koford 1963b), they do not always retain this high rank over a period of years (Table 13). Of the five young

TABLE 4

DOMINANCE INTERACTIONS BETWEEN SISTERS

1. Interactions between sisters which have both had at least one estrus period

Younger Sister Dominates Older Sister	Cases Observed	Older Sister Dominates Younger Sister	Cases Observed
XO dominates LA	12	SO9 dominates TN	1
YF dominates TI	1	ED dominates LU	1
NU dominates CS	1		
OP dominates JR	1		

2. Interactions between sisters one of which <u>has</u> <u>not</u> had an estrus period

Older Sister Dominates Younger Sister	Cases Observed		
LA dominates XO	9		
WF dominates A6	1		
JP dominates XJ	6		
YS dominates WP	1		
HJ dominates FM	1		

TABLE 5

DYADIC DOMINANCE INTERACTIONS IN GROUP A

Males

DW > S15', DX, EG, 79, 26', AN

IA > 26'', 79'', AN, JR, R, 81, S15

TP > KN, 62, 26'', XY, IX, 37, XA'', EG, 39'

26 > BY, JM, UZ, 15, LI, IV, YC, S15''', X, 62, 81

SO5 > S15', KH, GX, GA, ON, AL, FA

S15 > 81', DK, AL', HJ

AL > 64, 79, GX

79 > DV, XR, AN, NG, 15, 90, 106', DX, X, LI, JR, IX, DR, XA, EG

39 > DX, NG, 81'', EG

DK > DX'', 15, AN, GP, JE

DX > LH, 81, KN', FT, IX, EG', GO, NG', OG, UI, 15, JE

KN > HC

NJ > LD', YJ

NL > NQ

HC > IX'', S

IX > EG'''

YC > EG

EG > AL, XA'', FA, TV

LD > DV'', NP'', TP

NG > JA, FI

JA > NP', DV

NP > XY, NQ'', AN'', TF'', GW, XA

XA > NQ, ON

DV > AY, NQ

TABLE 5 Continued

Males (continued)

TQ > TF

TF > GW, NQ, ZB

NQ > AN, GW, XY

AN > DV, GW, ZP, 90

XY > GW

UT > GW

GW > AN, NQ

GO > BY, XR, ZD, 64

ZP > GZ, GX

L7 > ZD

ZD > Fl

GA > TV

Females

119 > 79, 106'', 81, 90, 07', LI'

UG > JR, JE, 15

GI > LH, X2, 07

JE > IA, 15''', 90', 64, 106'', GD, XR', UI''

AS > 106, JM

E7 > JM

81 > XP, 37, LH, OQ, JR, X''', TW

R10 > KH

07 > UI, GI

DR > XW, 15, TQ

GK > GY

X > 37, GO, TW, OP, JR, R, HP, 106

TABLE 5 <u>Continued</u>

<u>Females</u> (continued)

LH > TW, 37'

G3 > DV

37 > XR, JR, HP, TW

XR > LI''', UI

TW > DV

IV > 64', S, 15, 106, UI

AY > DV

GY > UI

UI > 15'', XR, OP, JR, TW

ZA > HJ

KH > HC

JH > FM', DZ

106 > XP, 15', BY

XP > 62, 90'

JM > YJ

RB > NJ

DZ > TV

JR > YJ, GO

TV > 37, TW, HP, TF

LH > YJ', OQ'

OP > JR, TV

OQ > DV

YJ > 106'', JR, OP

BP > 15

15 > TF', XY, WI, DR

TABLE 5 <u>Continued</u>

<u>Females</u> (continued)

S > HC

LI > BY, JO

R > DV

HS > ZD

Note: Primes denote number of times individual was dominated. Those without primes were dominated once. One prime means dominated twice, two primes mean dominated three times, etc.

TABLE 6

DYADIC DOMINANCE INTERACTIONS IN GROUP C

	Males																Females								
	27	DP	27	107	M	KV	121	EE	KT	EZ	ET	UE	NT	NY	XX	ZC	LN	BU	TX	RO5	KK	NF	AW	KK	DJ
Male 27		1		1					1		2						2								
DP			1	1		1		3	1								2	1							
107							1		1			1													
AG					1		1	1																	
CB					1																				
KT					1			2					1												
HO					3																				
M						1	1				1														
H3						1																			
113						1	1			1															
121								1																	
CV								1																	
AP								2																	
EZ														1											
UP											2														
UE															1										
YL													1												
UY															1										
XX																1									
Female AU	1																								
38																			1						
YO																				1					
NI																					1				
EW																						1			
HD																							1		
AT																								1	1

TABLE 7

DYADIC DOMINANCE INTERACTIONS IN GROUP E

	Males								Females																							
	IG	U	JX	JQ	TJ	YH	ZE	GF	EA	ED	LJ	OE	YF	TI	LW	114	WQ	24	NR	IS	I3	102	WP	UR	AJ	H8	128	S12	YS	YM	118	IR
Male																																
95		1							2																							
R15			1																													
U	1		1	1																												
JX		1		1			1																								1	
TB					1		1																									
YT																				1	1				1							1
ZE								1																								
Female																																
EA										3								1							1		1		1		1	
ED											1	2			2					1	1					1			1			
OE														1	2		1															
YF														1																		
TI																1																
LW																									1							
114																	1	2	1			2		1	1	1		1	1			1
WQ																									1	1				1		
IS																						1										
128																																
102																							1		1					1	1	
YS																							1							1		
YM							1																									

TABLE 8

DYADIC DOMINANCE INTERACTIONS IN GROUP F

	Males				Females		
	DS	JT	CN	WV	AC	22	JI
Male JS		1	1				
TD	1	1	1				1
JT			1			1	
CN				1			
WK					1		

TABLE 9

DYADIC DOMINANCE INTERACTIONS IN GROUP H

	Males					Females							
	KP	NE	NO	UU	ZO	84	S17	97	HT	49	AH	J8	XD
Male BC	2		1		3	2		1					
KP							1	3		1			1
NE			1										
NO				2	2								
UU					1							1	
ZO									1				
Female 84	2	1					5	1	2				
S17			3	2	1			5	2	1	1		1
97		1	4	1						6			
HT											1		
49													1

TABLE 10

DYADIC DOMINANCE INTERACTIONS IN GROUP I

	Males			Females					
	LT	J6	MC	AA	YI	116	NU	CS	CG
Male 96	1							1	1
LT							1		
Female 91				4		2			
AA					1				
YI		1	1						
IW			1						
116								1	
NU								1	

TABLE 11

DYADIC DOMINANCE INTERACTIONS IN GROUP J

	Males													Females											
	121	98	RO8	JQ	ES	UD	ZR	F7	F8	F4	K7	K8	L1	92	TN	SO9	XQ	LA	K9	T9	31	WF	XJ	JP	A6
Male 56	4	13	4	7	1	4	2		1	6				19	8	17	3	7	1	1	1	4	1	5	
121		8	6	9		1	6		1					5	9	8	7	7					3	6	
98			4	7	2	3	1		1					11	6	4		3	1		1	3	6	3	
RO8				1		5								4	13		5	6			2	4	4	6	
JQ						4	2									4	2	6				4	2	2	
ES															1						1				
ZR						2			1														1		
UD												1	1				2					3			1
F8								6										3				5			
Female 92			6	7		2	3	1	1						11	6	8	8	1		3	4	2	2	
TN			1	4			1	1	1	1						14	8				2	1		8	1
SO9			1	1		1			1						1		7	1			4	1	3	4	
XQ						2	3		2									12			3	2			
LA			1			7	2		1								9		2		3	4	1	23	1
K9											1	3	1												
31																	2	1					1	6	1
WF									1										1						1
XJ																	1								
JP			1			1	3						1		2		1	2					6		

TABLE 12

DOMINANCE INTERACTIONS IN WHICH COALITIONS WERE OBSERVED

Daughter + Mother

XW + 90, GC > HC

DR + 07 > DX

EA + MD > YS

Brothers

JA + NP > UD

Sisters

TN + SO9 > JP

Aunt + Niece

TN + XQ > 31

Son enlists Mother + Aunt

ZR, SO9 + TN > UD

No Known Relationship

HC + 39 > IX

AY + 12 > DV

GX + GO > 64

No Relationship

NP + NQ > AN

JP + 92 > RO8

LV + TW > 37

TABLE 13

CHANGES IN DOMINANCE RANK OF TEN HIGHEST RANKING MALES IN GROUP A FROM
JUNE 1962 TO AUGUST 1967

Ranks in June 1962 from Koford (1963b), December 1962-September 1963
from Kaufmann (1967), and August 1967 (Wilson)

Male	Rank in June 1962	Rank in Dec. 1962	Rank in Feb-Apr 1963	Rank in July 1963	Rank in Sept. 1963	Rank in Aug. 1967
14	1	1	1	1	3	0*
S07	2	0[†]	0	0	0	0[†]
DW	3	2	2	2	1	1
DV	4	3	3	3	2	24[‡]
56	5	4	4	4	4	0[†]
26	6	5	6	6	6	4
08	7	6	7	7	7	0[†]
79	8	7	8	8	8	8
121	9	8	0[†]	0	9[§]	0[†]
98	10	0[†]	0	0	0	0[†]

* Missing, presumed dead.

† Left group.

‡ Periphery.

§ Returned to group.

high-ranking males (4 to 6 years old) listed by Koford as occupying second or third dominance rank in their respective groups in 1962, and whose mothers were the highest ranking females of the group, one has subsequently been removed from Cayo Santiago, one has become the dominant male in his natal group, and three have left their natal groups; in the new groups they are not the highest-ranking males nor do they continue to outrank younger males.

Sade (1967) pointed out that as males become adult they tend to rank near their mothers in the adult hierarchy in the group, but at puberty or later, if they remain in the group, they may gain or lose rank. He speculates that around the time of puberty or later, the physiological differences between males become more important than fighting in determining dominance rank, and that the differences that derive from past experience and continued association with adults of different rank become less overriding.

All observed changes of dominance rank among high-ranking males occurred during the mating season (see Table 14), and it was also at this time that males were most likely to change groups. Koford (1966) pointed out that 66% of male departures from groups of membership during the years 1960 to 1964 occurred from August to November, the period of greatest mating activity. Males which joined new groups invariably were observed to take up dominance positions near the bottom of the adult male hierarchy in the new group.

While males below the age of six years may rise quickly to high rank and then fall in rank, this does not happen invariably. Male DW, the dominant male of Group A, became group leader at the age of five years and has maintained his position for over five years. However,

TABLE 14

OBSERVED CHANGES IN MALE DOMINANCE STATUS

Group A (Koford 1963a)	(Kaufmann 1967)				(Wilson)
June 1962	Dec. 1962	Feb.-April 1963	July 1963	Sept. 1963	Aug. 1967
14	14	14	14	DW	DW
SO7	DW	DW	DW	DV	IA
DW	DV	DV	DV	14	TP
DV	56	56	56	56	26
56	26	EY	EY	EY	SO5
26	08	26	26	26	S15
08	79	08	08	08	AL
79	121	79	79	79	79
121	SO5	TA	IA	121	39
98	AL	EP	121 DS,KU,EP,KX	SO5	DK
	BA	AL	SO5	IA	DX
	DX	BA	AL	EP	KN
	113	BZ	BA	AL	NJ
	AV	DX	BZ	BA	NL
	EG	113	DX	DX	HC
	AN	AV	AV	AV	IX
	KN	EG	AN	AN	YC
	53?	AN	53	53	EG
	KB	KN	KB	KB	LD
	CZ	53?	EG	EG	NG
	DK	KB	KN	KN	JA
		CZ	CZ	CZ	NP
		DK	DK	DK	XA
			113	113	DV
					TQ
					TF
					NQ
					AN
					XY
					UT
					GW
					GO
					ZP
					L7
					ZD
					GA

TABLE 14 Continued

Group C

(Koford 1963)	(Wilson)
June 1962	August 1967
JF	27
E5	DP
103	107
KC	AG
132	CB
63	KT
05	HO
27	M
06	H3
01	113
	121
	CV
	AP
	EZ
	UP
	UE
	YL
	UY
	XX

Group E

CL	95
95	R15
R15	U
R06	JX
EJ	TB
BC	YT
BD	ZE

TABLE 14 <u>Continued</u>

Group F

(Koford 1963b)	(Sade 1967)			(Wilson)
	All Months			
June 1962	1961	1962	1963	1967
66	Old Male A	Old Male A 066	Old Male A 066	RO6
RO8	1956 Male 1 RO8	1956 Male 1 RO8	1957 Male 4 ER	
CN	1956 Male B 053	1957 Male 4 ER	1956 Male C 019	
ER	1956 Male 5 CN	1956 Male 5 CN	1958 Male 6 CY	
CY			1965 Male 5 B4	

at least since 1965, the dominant males in Groups E, F, H, I, and J are the oldest males or at least as old as any other male in each group. The ages of the males are given in Table 26 (Appendix A), and the dominance positions are given in Tables 5-11.

Only three triangular dominance relationships were seen. These occurred in August 1967 and are shown in Table 15. One triangle was observed among the lowest ranking males in Group A; the other two occurred among the highest ranking males in the same group. These triangular relationships were probably temporary as they occurred during the onset of the mating season, when dominance relationships are in greatest flux.

Some adult females are dominant to adult males. Usually such females are from high-ranking lines and over ten years old. These interactions are included in Tables 5-11.

Dominance relations between males were often not related to physical size. Adult males were often subordinate to subadult males half their weight. No quantitative data are available, however, since estimates of weight were made from observation only and based on earlier measurements of weight made for monkeys of known age at Cayo Santiago.

E. Seasonal Fluctuations in Wounds (August 1965 to August 1967)

Wounds were noted during census-taking by Mr. Angel Figueroa (cited here with the permission of Dr. Myers) and during my own observations. Any visible cut, usually 4 cm or longer, was noted. Wound frequencies may have been underestimated during the months of July and August due to the press of other duties, illness and vacation of Mr. Figueroa during those months in both 1966 and 1967. This may be

TABLE 15

TRIANGULAR DOMINANCE RELATIONSHIPS OF MALES IN AUGUST 1967

DV > NQ

AN > DV

NQ > AN

79 > EG

EG > AL

AL > 79

Explanation: DV once 3rd ranking. Now low-ranking peripheral and NQ is about 14 lbs. weight. DV over 25 lbs. AN is also over 25 lbs. AN came into group after NQ.

responsible for the fact that both Sade (1966) and Kaufmann (1967) conclude that aggression is more pronounced in the period between birth and mating seasons while wound frequencies are greatest during the mating season.

Wounding of males was significantly increased during the mating season (X^2 = 25, P < .001). However, while the wounding of females also increased during the mating season this difference was not significant (X^2 = .87, P > .30). While the sample size was not great enough to show a statistical difference, a larger number of sexually mature monkeys of both sexes were wounded than immatures (see Table 16).

F. Seasonal Fluctuation in Mortality

Between August 1965 and August 1967, thirty-one recorded deaths occurred at Cayo Santiago. Untattooed infants less than three months old that died before being noted on the census sheets were not included in the death records. Therefore, this section does not cover infant mortality before the age of three months. Koford (1966) described the Cayo Santiago mortality data from the standpoint of the age of death. This section is concerned only with the seasonality of death (which was not covered by Koford). Mortality of males was found to be significantly greater during the mating season (X^2 = 11, P < .001); however, the mortality of females was not correlated with either the mating or nonmating season (X^2 = 2.2, P > .1) (see Table 17). Mortality of monkeys at Cayo Santiago is due primarily to infections arising from wounds received in fighting (John A. Morrison, personal communication).

Due to the size of the population and the fact that only one man, Mr. Angel Figueroa, is responsible for censusing, the exact month of

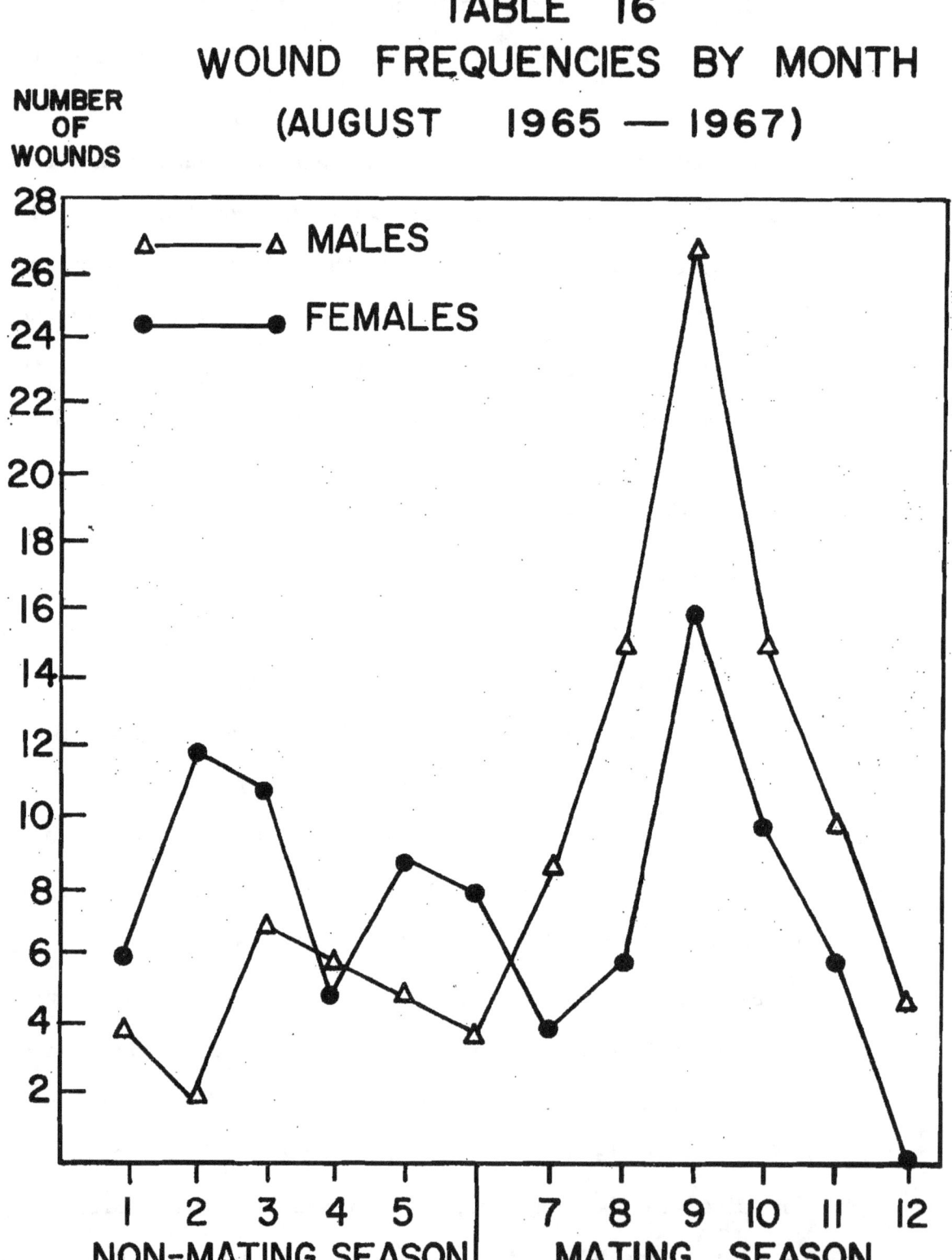

TABLE 16
WOUND FREQUENCIES BY MONTH
(AUGUST 1965 — 1967)

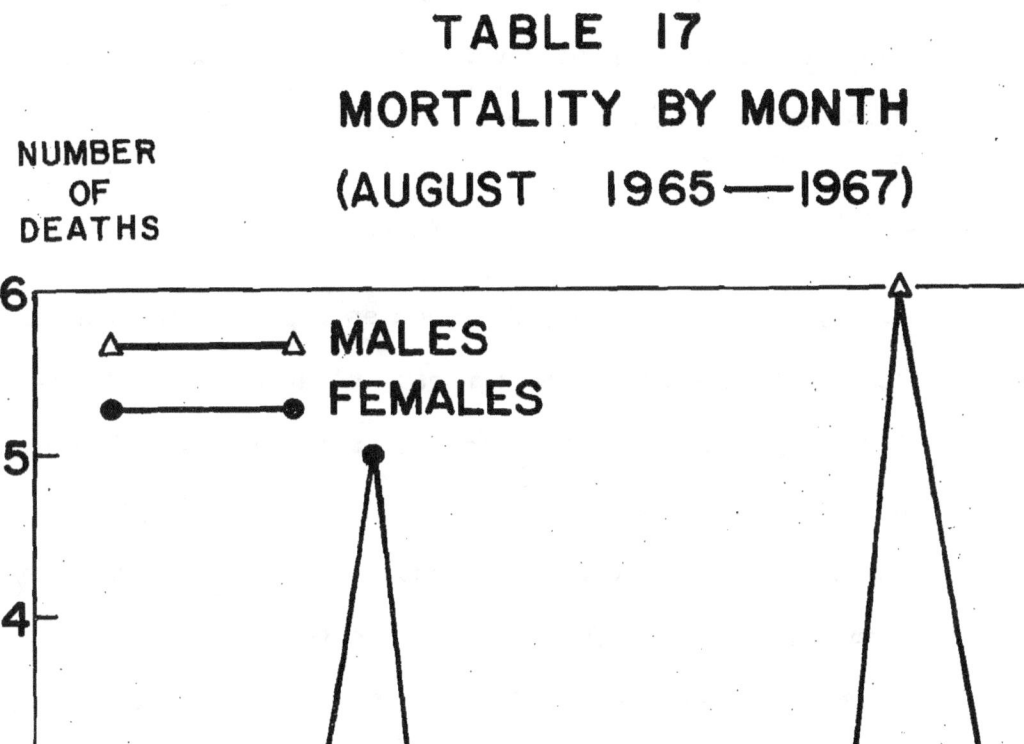

TABLE 17
MORTALITY BY MONTH
(AUGUST 1965—1967)

NUMBER
OF
DEATHS

△——△ MALES
●——● FEMALES

NON-MATING SEASON | MATING SEASON

death is not known for most monkeys. A complete census of all monkeys
is possible only about once a month. Mr. Figueroa also has other care-
taking duties which take time away from his observations and thus some
monkeys may be missing for over a month before they are recorded as
dead. Thus, for example, a monkey which was recorded as dead in November may have died in September or possibly even in late August.

G. Discussion

Mortality rates, wounding, frequencies of agonistic behavior,
and dominance rank changes in male rhesus monkeys are all more pronounced during the mating period and decrease during the birth period.
The heightened aggression of the mating period is accompanied by changes
in gonadal physiology. Increases in testis size (Sade 1964) and spermato-
genesis (Conaway and Sade 1965) have been noted at Cayo Santiago during
the mating period; Vandenberg (1965), on the basis of laboratory studies,
suggested that testosterone levels also rise at this time and decrease
during the birth season. However, while the male hormone testosterone
has been noted to facilitate aggression in many vertebrate species
(Collias 1944), Klopper (1964) found the effects of male hormones on
primate aggression difficult to evaluate. One rhesus male castrate
observed by Zuckerman and Parkes (1938) became "fiercer and more dominant"
when injected with testosterone. On the other hand, when Mirsky (1955)
injected five rhesus male castrates with testosterone he did not see any
change in dominance. The dosage used by Mirsky, however, was one-third
that used by Vandenberg (1965) to approximate testosterone levels at
Cayo Santiago during the mating season. Thus the facilitating effect
of testosterone on male aggression and competition for dominance in

rhesus monkeys cannot be ruled out until Mirsky's experiment is repeated using the higher dosage.

Observations of ten rhesus monkey male castrates living among free-ranging groups at Cayo Santiago and at the La Parguera rhesus monkey colony were reported by Wilson and Vessey (in press). Pronounced individual differences in aggression were seen and these were related in part to affectional ties with other monkeys. Although no castrate was a high-ranking male in its group, two prepubertally castrated males fought and dominated males twice their weight. Six postpubertally castrated males gradually fell in dominance rank several years after castration. One genotypic male born without either male or female sex organs (described morphologically by Koford, Farber, and Windle 1966) behaved as a low-ranking male in Group C.

The high level of male fighting during the mating season was most pronounced at dusk or shortly after sunset, as noted in Chapter II. Identification of individuals is difficult to make during this period; however, the forms of the monkeys and their agonistic vocalizations are quite apparent. Because aggression is most pronounced when observations are most difficult, wound and mortality data are a useful supplement to diurnal observations concerning the severity of agonistic behavior. Monkeys at Cayo Santiago have been shown to be relatively free of infectious disease.

While high-ranking males have been observed to mate more often than low-ranking males at Cayo Santiago (Kaufmann 1965), no intragroup fighting over females has been noted. However, as a consequence of fighting that occurs during and shortly before the breeding season, the strongest males are selected as the most dominant, and hence they contribute more to the genetic composition of the population.

Five group divisions have been noted at Cayo Santiago (see Chapter I), all of which occurred during the mating season. It may be adaptive for group fission to occur at that time in the natural habitat so that new territories may be explored prior to the birth season, when females and infants are more vulnerable than during other periods of the year. Heightened aggression between males during the mating season may facilitate group fission; however, no group fission was observed during the period of this study. Heightened tensions between males may also be partially responsible for the high rate of group switching by males during the mating season (Koford 1966).

Both mortality and wounds of females show peaks during the birth and mating seasons (see Tables 16 and 17). The mortality peak during the birth season might be attributed in part to deaths due to difficulties in giving birth. The fact that wound frequencies are also high, however, indicates that aggression may also be responsible for increased mortality during the birth season. It is interesting to note that while there is no significant seasonal difference between wound and mortality frequencies in females, there is in males. This indicates that aggression directed toward females does not correlate with the mating season as it does with males. Carpenter (1942), Altmann (1962), and Southwick (1965) have indicated that rhesus monkey females tend to become more aggressive about the time of estrus. However, the complex hormonal changes that occur during estrus, pregnancy, and nursing have not been clearly related to aggression. Kaufmann (1965) found that there was no consistent correlation between rank and sexual activity of females, in contrast to a positive correlation for males. While the data are not yet conclusive, it appears that females rise in dominance rank over their older

sisters (Sade 1967) when they reach their first estrus period at the
beginning of the mating season. Otherwise, adult female dominance
rank is extremely stable, in contrast to dominance relations of adult
males.

In conclusion, it appears that aggressive and reproductive behaviors
of rhesus monkeys at Cayo Santiago are associated seasonally. This
supports the observations made on this species in their native habitat,
India (Lindburg 1966, Neville 1966, Southwick 1965).

IV. INTERGROUP RELATIONS WITH AN EMPHASIS ON MALE INTERGROUP TRANSFER

A. Introduction

In this chapter, agonistic and nonagonistic social relations between groups are described with particular attention to the role of
long-term social ties in the process of male intergroup transfer. Because of the unique nature of this island colony with its abnormally
high population density compared with rhesus monkeys in their natural
habitat (Neville 1968), the relationship of group dispersion patterns
at Cayo Santiago to territoriality may be of limited significance for
those interested in the comparison of the colony with rhesus monkeys
in India. The dispersion of the groups at Cayo Santiago was described
in Chapter I. Intergroup male transfer has been noted in Indian rhesus
monkeys (Lindburg 1966, Southwick 1965) and the observations of such
transfers at Cayo Santiago may give some idea concerning the various
ways such transfers are accomplished.

B. Agonistic Intergroup Behavior

Agonistic behavior between groups occurred most frequently near
the feeders. Out of 112 observed intergroup supplanting interactions,
only 13 took place away from the feeders (see Table 18). An intergroup
supplanting interaction was considered to have taken place when a portion of a group containing adult males, adult females, and subadult
monkeys spatially displaced a similar portion of another group. This
definition was needed to separate such intergroup agonistic behavior
from interactions between several monkeys separated from their group
with larger numbers of monkeys from other groups.

TABLE 18

SUPPLANTING INTERACTIONS BETWEEN IDENTIFIED GROUPS, (+) WITH COMBAT, (−) WITHOUT COMBAT

I. At the Feeders

	C +	C −	A +	A −	E +	E −	F +	F −	H +	H −	I +	I −	J +	J −	Total +	Total −
C				4		3	3	3			1	3	1	12	5	25
A	1	2				1						1		6	1	10
E								4		2				7		13
F				1						2	1	2		9	1	14
H		1												8		9
I		2								1				4		7
J				1		3				4		4	2		2	12
Total	1	5		6		7	3	7		9	2	10	3	46	9	90

II. Away from the Feeders

	C +	C −	A +	A −	E +	E −	F +	F −	H +	H −	I +	I −	J +	J −	Total +	Total −
C												2		1		3
A					1									3	1	3
E								1						2		3
F														2		2
H																
I																
J										1						1
Total					1			1		1		2		8	1	12

Of 112 intergroup supplantations that were observed, only ten involved contact. By contact I refer to physical contact between combatants. While agonistic display was common in intergroup encounters, fighting with contact was rarely observed between groups. My observations may be misleading on this point, however, because most of the serious fighting took place at dusk when identification of the individual combatants was rarely possible. Males and females from the age of two years on were observed in agonistic intergroup encounters. Low-ranking adult and subadult males were the most frequent combatants in intergroup agonistic display or combat, although they could not all be individually identified.

The groups may be ranked in dominance on the basis of supplantations according to size: C, A, E, F, H, I, J. However, this is not an absolute dominance hierarchy since smaller groups do occasionally supplant larger groups.

Intergroup agonistic encounters involving male subgroups and individual males with other groups are quite variable. In some cases, only one male of a high-ranking group was sufficient to supplant an entire low-ranking group. In other cases, low-ranking groups supplanted individual males or subgroups from larger groups (see Table 19). Generally, high-ranking males from high-ranking groups could by themselves supplant low-ranking groups, while low-ranking males from high-ranking groups acting alone or in subgroups of less than five individuals were not able to supplant low-ranking groups. For example, male 113, the alpha male of Group C, was seen to supplant Group A by himself at a feeder. However, three females of Group F chased two low-ranking Group C males, UE and YV, away from Group F. Particularly during the mating season, males

TABLE 19

INTERGROUP INDIVIDUAL DOMINANCE INTERACTIONS

NE > LG	JI > UP
97 > WC	JQ > 113
CV > 53	121 > AN
UD > N6 + UU	95 > DX
UB > DV	DV > 98 + J group
KN > LA	JX > JT + J group
JS > IU	56 > WR
98 > XT, OB, ZC, YC	JX > JQ
ES > XT, OB, ZC, YC	GO > XJ
JP > WC	

leave their groups and approach the periphery of new groups where they are often chased away.

C. The Relationship of Grooming and Association to Nonagonistic Social Relations

Sade (1965) and Kaufmann (1966, 1967) have made excellent studies concerning the ontogeny of nonagonistic social relations at Cayo Santiago. Naturally, their work stresses the relationship between nonagonistic relations and genealogical information available at Cayo Santiago. Sade and Kaufmann each reported on one group at Cayo Santiago, Sade on Group F and Kaufmann on Group A. Therefore, in an attempt not to duplicate this previous work, I will stress affectional ties which are related to intergroup relations.

Sade (1965) found that social relations within a group were identified "by the consistent close spacing of particular monkeys, by the choices of partners which monkeys make for various activities, and by incidents, some of which occur too infrequently to provide much quantitative information but which often show the fact of the relation." Sade used "spacing" and "grooming" as his quantitative data indicating affectional ties. As an index of close spacing, Sade tabulated the times that one individual was observed sitting or lying close to another. Sade noted that "Of any single kind of activity grooming is best suited for demonstrating relations between animals of different sex and ages." Sade's tabulations of grooming showed the relative frequency with which particular individuals chose and were accepted by certain other individuals as grooming partners, but his report did not include information on the duration of the counted bouts of grooming. "In order to time a bout I had to see it begin, then watch nothing else until it ended, but usually I came upon monkeys already grooming and had no idea how long the bout already had lasted. As often as not bouts were ended by disturbances; the length of such bouts depends more upon the length of time the partners were left alone than on the strength of their grooming relation [italics mine]. Nevertheless, the longer a bout lasted the more likely it was that I would see part of it as I wandered about, and the tabulations may in fact be weighted on the side of relations characterized by longer bouts. The tabulations give no hint as to the context in which the bouts occurred." The infrequent incidents to which Sade refers are primarily coalitions in the context of agonistic encounters which indicate close social relations. Such relationships are described in Appendix B.

Kaufmann (1967) noted that "Grooming is probably the most important social act for revealing rhesus band organization." Kaufmann, like Sade, used "spacing" and "grooming" as his primary criteria for non-agonistic social relations. He introduced the term "associates" to refer to monkeys located within 20 feet of each other during "stable" situations. Kaufmann's data are concerned largely with the age-sex-rank categories of "associates" and they emphasize the associations of adult males with other monkeys. His grooming tabulations are essentially the same as Sade's.

My own observations have supported Sade's and Kaufmann's use of grooming and association as the most easily observable and frequent nonagonistic social behaviors. However, it does happen that monkeys are spatially close, in fact are touching, when they are grooming and therefore frequency of grooming is an index of frequency of spatial

closeness and vice versa. Among females, grooming between associates
was so frequent that I felt it was not necessary to include data on
spatial propinquity to adequately gauge affectional ties. Among males
three years of age and older, however, grooming was relatively infrequent and it became important to note spatial propinquity along with
grooming in order to describe male associations. While this sparse set
of criteria for social ties may be unsatisfactory for describing the
details of affectional behavior among the monkeys, the catalogue presented in the appendix may be of help in this regard. By using grooming
relationships and associations as my primary indexes of nonagonistic
social relations (as did Sade and Kaufmann), it was possible for me to
survey more animals in a shorter period of time than by any other method.

D. Nonagonistic Intergroup Relations

The nonagonistic intergroup behavior consisted of intergroup grooming (male:male and female:female), sitting within 20 feet of another
group for over 10 minutes, and copulations between males and females
belonging to different groups. While copulations as a factor in reproductive behavior have been described by Conaway and Koford (1965) and
by Kaufmann (1965), I am including my observations of intergroup copulations as a part of rare intergroup nonagonistic relations between males
and females not described previously at Cayo Santiago.

It may be that intergroup grooming is infrequently seen because
the presence of a human observer tends to make the monkeys less willing
to engage in friendly intergroup contacts. In four out of five cases
of intergroup grooming between a male and a female, no agonistic behavior
on the part of members belonging to either group was seen. In two out

of three intergroup grooming interactions between males no agonistic behavior on the part of members belonging to either group was noted. Observations of intergroup grooming are summarized as follows:

♀:♂ 20 July 1965. Ten-year-old female RO2 of Group H grooms nine-year-old male 98 of Group J. The pair is alone in the bushes. After 3 minutes of observation the rest of Group J approaches. As ten-year-old male 121 comes within 2 meters of the pair, female RO2 runs off as male 121 chases her away. Then male 121 returns and male 98 bobs and directs an open mouth threat toward male 121. However, male 121 does not acknowledge male 98's threat (121 > 98). Male 121 then walks into the bushes followed by male 98. Male 98 then goes up to male 121 and grooms him for 15 minutes.

♀:♂ 30 August 1965. Three-year-old female TN of Group J was observed grooming an unidentified adult male for 1 hour while sitting in a tree 4 meters above other Group J monkeys. No reaction of other group members to the extra group male was seen up to the time observation was terminated.

♂:♂ 10 October 1965. Five-year-old male JV of Group C grooms with three-year-old male XT of Group A for 5 minutes when observation was terminated.

♂:♂ 1 November 1966. Three-year-old male UD of Group J grooms unidentified adult male sitting 20 feet from Group J for over 15 minutes when observation was terminated. No Group J members paid any attention to the extra-group male.

♂:♂ 29 November 1966. Twelve-year-old male SO7 of Group I grooms nine-year-old male 98 of Group J for 10 minutes as both groups sit 10 feet apart. Male 98 then attacks and bites male SO7 as females from the two groups begin to threaten each other.

♂:♀ 4 April 1967. Members of Groups C, A, and E sit peacefully inter-
♂:♀ mixed with each other near feeder 5. (Observations were made be-
tween 1500 and 1525 hours.) Twelve-year-old male 95, the dominant male of Group E, chases ten-year-old male AL of Group A for 2 meters, then male 95 walks away as AL sits and grooms eight-year-old female DJ of Group C. Five-year-old female OP of Group A walks up to and grooms male 95 as eleven-year-old male 79 of Group A sits quietly 1 meter from the grooming pair for over 5 minutes.

♀:♂ 1 May 1967. Group J sits 1 meter from Group F. Three-year-old
♀:♀ female FB of Group F grooms five-year-old male UD and his sister, three-year-old female WF of Group J, as twelve-year-old male RO6, the dominant male of Group F, sits quietly, 1 meter from the groom-ing monkeys. After 10 minutes Groups F and J move apart peace-fully.

♀:♂ 30 August 1965. Three-year-old female TN grooms unidentified adult solitary male. Group J members are grooming nearby under the man-groves. Both TN and the male sit in a mangrove tree about 4 meters off the ground over other members of Group J. TN grooms the male for over an hour when observation was terminated.

While individual monkeys, particularly males, were often seen near other groups, a prolonged spatial propinquity of the main body of several groups (including high-ranking males, females and offspring) was rare. These interactions are summarized in Table 20.

TABLE 20

GROUPS SITTING WITHIN 20 FEET OF EACH OTHER FOR
OVER 10 MINUTES, AWAY FROM FEEDERS

Time	Date	Groups
1825	4 July 1967	E, J
1500	4 April 1967	C, A, E
1900	20 February 1967	C, F
1800	5 December 1967	F, A, J
1615	8 November 1966	C, J
1830	14 August 1967	A, C
1730	19 July 1967	E, J
1040	20 July 1965	J, H
0800	29 July 1965	I, J

The majority of copulations observed at Cayo Santiago were between males and females belonging to the same group (Kaufmann 1965). Intergroup copulations are summarized as follows:

11 August 1965, 0720-0730: Nine-year-old male 98 of Group J mounts six-year-old female CS of Group I. Group J members are sitting and grooming near feeder 3 which is empty. Female CS approaches Group J. Male 98 walks toward female CS. Female CS turns and walks away from Group J with male 98 following her. They stop about 12 meters away from Group J. Male 98 mounts female CS and delivers 12 pelvic thrusts while female CS

looks back at him and grimaces. Male 98 dismounts and sits. Female CS walks 20 feet away from male 98 and then looks back at him. Male 98 walks over to female CS and slaps her on the back. Female CS runs away to a spot about 20 feet away from male 98 and looks back at male 98 again. Male 98 walks over to female CS, mounts her, delivers 12 pelvic thrusts while grimacing. Female CS grimaces back at male 98. Male 98 dismounts and both monkeys sit touching each other. Eleven-year-old male 56 (the dominant male of Group J) runs over toward the sitting couple and chases female CS out of sight. Then male 56 returns to sit on the spot where female CS was sitting. Male 98 moves a few feet away and proceeds to groom himself. The other members of Group J join male 56 and male 98. Group I moves to sit about 10 meters from Group J. Female CS sits with the Group I members. Male 98 sits for several minutes grooming himself. Then male 21 walks over to ten-year-old male RO8, also a Group J member. Male RO8 is sitting on the ground about 3 meters from where male 98 had been self-grooming. Male 98 places his right forelimb on male RO8's back for about 30 seconds, then sits down beside him. They sit touching for about 2 minutes. Then male 98 gets up and walks away. Male RO8 begins to groom himself.

20 August 1965, 0925-0935: Ten-year-old male 21 of Group J mounts six-year-old female EL of Group C. Group J is feeding at feeder 3. Female EL is sitting about 30 feet away from the feeder. Male 21 approaches female EL and mounts her delivering six pelvic thrusts. He dismounts and they both sit quietly for 30 seconds. Then male 21 mounts again and delivers 16 pelvic thrusts. One-year-old male ZR walks over to the couple. Male 21 dismounts and chases male ZR out of sight. Female EL walks away.

5 December 1966, 1700-1750: Eleven-year-old male 121 of Group C (formerly of Group J) mounts seven-year-old female CS, four-year-old female NU, two-year-old female XC; the females are all members of Group I and sisters. Members of Groups A, C, E, F, and I are inter-mingled near feeder 6. An unidentified adult female mounts another unidentified adult female and delivers eleven pelvic thrusts. (Fights between monkeys of various ages occur with great frequency--about one fight per 3 minutes is noted.) Male 121 (a low-ranking male) of Group C fights with and causes male DW (the dominant male of Group A) to flee. No monkeys from Group A come to DW's aid. Then male 121 mounts female CS of Group I and gives 15 thrusts. Male 121 mounts CS again three times in rapid succession giving 10, 17, and 10 thrusts respectively as the dominant male of Group I (96) sits 3 meters from the copulating pair looking on impassively. Three-year-old female IW of Group I then threatens female CS and CS threatens back. An unidentified adult male rushes up to fight with three unidentified Group I females near female CS and male 121 who run off in separate directions. Then male 121 returns and mounts female NU, gives five thrusts and ejaculates leaving a vaginal plug. Then male 121 goes up to female XC, mounts, and gives seven thrusts while male 96 sits 1 meter from the pair. Male 121 then walks over to two-year-old female TO who sits on her haunches grimacing and as he walks to her rear she turns in a circle to continue facing him while she remains sitting. Male 121 grabs female TO's tail and yanks her up into position to be mounted; however, female TO runs off screaming. Then male 121 runs off into the brush.

E. Intergroup Male Transfer

Kaufmann (1967) has dealt with the intergroup associations of males in Group A. His principal concern was with rank and age related to associations. My concern was with the long-term affectional ties of males, as these associations were related to intergroup relations.

Intergroup transfer has been reported in rhesus monkeys in India by Southwick (1965) and Lindburg (1966), and at Cayo Santiago by Altmann (1962) and Koford (1966). These studies indicate that rhesus male monkeys change groups more frequently than females and thus Koford points out that males rather than females are the primary sources of genetic exchange between different groups inhabiting a region.

Altmann (1962) reported that during the period 1956 to 1958 (at this time there were only two groups on the island) he observed only one permanent change in group membership at Cayo Santiago and it was made by a three-year-old male. Five other males and two females were seen in temporary association with monkeys not belonging to their own group.

Koford reported that between 1959 and 1963, 151 changes in group membership were made which lasted more than one month; 91% of these changes were made by males. During this period, the population rose from 227 to 482 monkeys and the number of social groups on the island expanded from two to six. The ages at which males changed group status during Koford's study ranged from two years to over seven years. Infant and yearling males never changed groups and two-year-olds rarely changed unless their mothers did. Of all males at least three years old, 301 changes in group status were noted. These changes involved 78 males of which about a fourth shifted in more than one of the years of Koford's study. A similar proportion changed membership more than once a year, and two males spent a month or more in four different groups over a period of three or four years. Over 66% of male departures from groups occurred from August to November, the height of the mating season; Koford noted that this period is characterized by frequent fighting.

From March 1965 to September 1967, 63 changes in group membership by 52 males were observed at Cayo Santiago. During this period, four males changed group membership twice, one changed three times and one changed five times. The remaining 46 males only changed groups once. As Table 21 indicates, Koford's observations that yearlings and infants never change groups, that two-year-old males rarely change groups, and that most membership changes occur during the mating season are supported by this more recent data.

As Table 21 indicates, males are much more likely to join the two largest groups on the island and less likely to join the five smallest groups (x^2 = 70, P < .001). This may be due to the fact that the two largest groups, A and C, both have peripheral male subgroups and the smaller groups do not. My observations indicate that extra group males are tolerated by these male subgroups to a greater extent than hetero-sexual groups tolerate them. Composition of these male subgroups changes daily; they may vary in size from five to over 20 males. Solitary males and males from the central group may join the male subgroups for hours or days and then drift off. When males are observed consistently staying with a subgroup they are considered to be members of that group.

TABLE 21

CHANGES IN GROUP MEMBERSHIP, MARCH 1965-SEPTEMBER 1967
WHICH LASTED MORE THAN ONE MONTH

Age of Change to Nearest Year	Number of Changes in Group Status in Each Age Class	Groups to Which Change Was Made
1	0	
2	1	C
3	14	C = 11 A = 3
4	17	A = 10 E = 3 I = 2 H = 1 C = 1
5	4	C = 2 H = 1 Solitary = 1
6	3	A = 1 C = 1 Solitary = 1
7	5	C = 2 Solitary = 3
8	6	A = 5 C = 1
9	4	A = 1 C = 1 Solitary = 2
10	3	A = 1 C = 1 E = 1
11	4	A = 1 E = 1 J = 1 Solitary = 1
12	1	A = 1
13	0	
14	0	
15	1	E = 1
+15	0	

63 total number of changes in group membership

52 = number of males observed changing group status

Month of Change	Number of Changes in Each Month	Number of Changes to Each Group
January	5	A = 23
February	0	C = 21
March	1	E = 6
April	4	F = 0
May	3	I = 2
June	1	H = 2
July	0	J = 1
August	11	
September	24	Solitary = 8
October	5	
November	7	
December	1	

F. Integration of Males into a New Group

The process of transferring into subgroups or into the other groups on the island has not previously been described. Indeed this is a variable process for each male that comes into the group, and therefore it is not easily amenable to quantitative behavioral description. I have observed the integration of several males into new groups and have noted a few patterns by which this is achieved.

Over 68% of the males observed joining a new group picked either Group A or Group C. These are the two largest groups on Cayo Santiago with close to two hundred monkeys in each group.

These groups both have peripheral male subgroups which the five smaller groups do not have. The peripheral male subgroups are highly variable in membership from day to day. Sometimes the peripheral males in both groups were observed in two or three spatially distinct male subgroups. Thus one subgroup of five peripheral Group A males might be located near feeder 3 on the Small Cay at the same time that another seven peripheral males of Group A forages near the boat landing. Sub-groups of peripheral males were observed ranging in size from two to over 20 members. These subgroups often ranged far from their respective central groups. Kaufmann (1967) found, as I did, that peripheral male subgroups are largest in membership during the nonbreeding season.

These peripheral male subgroups are the most popular groups for males to change to particularly for the two-, three-, and four-year-old males leaving their natal group for the first time (see Table 21). One way in which these males manage to become accepted into the new group is by forming an association with a male which is already a member of the group. The association between a subgroup member and a male attempting to enter the subgroup is characterized by extensive mutual grooming by the pair and by support of the extra-group male by the subgroup member in agonistic encounters with other monkeys. This sponsor-protégé pair may stay close together for a period of time ranging from several days to months in duration. However, the relationship of this pair does not exclude affectional social contacts such as grooming and play between the individual monkeys in the pair and other monkeys in the subgroup. Sometimes one monkey in such an associated pair strikes up a special association with a third male. Such a third male attached to a "friendship-pair" of two associated males often is the butt of redirected aggression when the males in the subgroup are excited or stressed for any reason. Although I have closely followed the integration of only two four-year-old males and one three-year-old male from the first week of transfer over a period of more than seven months, I feel that most males under five years of age joining new groups are integrated in this manner. These males, particularly the males that are four years old and younger could be easily driven away from the peripheral male subgroups by older subgroup members. Males in the subgroups range from two to over 15 years of age.

It may be that young males find it easier to be assimilated into the peripheral male subgroups than into the central part of Groups A and C or the five smaller groups on the island. Whether or not the absence of females from the subgroups facilitates integration of males into the subgroups was not determined.

The males which join new groups by forming associations with males that are already group members often form associations with males that

have previously resided in the natal group of the extra-group male.
For example, a male joining a new group may form an "association" with
its brother which left the natal group and joined a new group several
years previously. Sade (in press) reports on three such fraternal
associations outside of the natal group by brothers born into Group F.
He also notes a younger brother joining his two older brothers in a
new group. My data also indicate that <u>all</u> brothers (three pairs) that
were members of the same nonnatal group were close associates and that
genealogically unrelated males born in the same natal group but residing in a nonnatal group were often close associates (see Table 22).

Three males over five years old were observed during the initial
week of their transfer into a new group. One of these (male 19) was
not observed forming associations with males in the group (Group J),
but rather followed the group and was observed sitting and grooming
with females. One adult male (AN), a former member of Group A, rejoined
the peripheral subgroup of Group A, and was not observed in friendly
interaction with the males in that subgroup. Each of these three males
was observed for about 2 hours over a period of 4 days during the initial
period of transfer. It is possible that males younger than five years
of age may enter new groups without forming close male associations;
however, only males five years of age and older were observed joining
new groups in this fashion.

G. The <u>Significance</u> of <u>Intergroup</u> <u>Male</u> <u>Transfer</u> <u>for</u>
    <u>Intergroup</u> <u>Social</u> <u>Relations</u>

As Table 23 indicates, the percentage of males in each age class
born in their groups of membership drops sharply from almost 100% for

TABLE 22

MALE ASSOCIATIONS: OBSERVATIONS OF MALES ASSOCIATING FOR TIME PERIODS OF 5 MINUTES AND OVER*

Related in non-natal group†	Related in natal group	Nonrelated living in nonnatal group but born in same natal group		Nonrelated living in natal group	Nonrelated living in nonnatal group and born in different natal groups	Male living in natal group with male born in another group	Genealogy and natal group unknown for one of males
YV,UE(br)(3)	NZ,OW(br)	XT,ZC(1)	FA,NG	ZE,TB	XT,YA	ET,AG	ES,AN
YA,NT(br)(9)	UD,LI(uncle, nephew)	OB,YC	NL,UP	NJ,GZ	NT,YV	G5,EG	19,ES,DK
JA,NP(br)(5)	ZR,F8(br)	XL,XT(1)	HC,FA	FP,TD	YV,YA	JX,ZE	XY,AN(1)
	UD,F4(uncle, nephew)	YV,UY	UE,XT	NO,UU	ZC,NT	FT,UP	NP,AN
	F4,LI(br)	ZC,XX	EG,HC	TP,GX	NP,TF	DX,NG	AN,X
		XL,YV	XY,EG	AG,ET	HC,IX(1)	UT,FT	EG,79
		ZC,XL,XT,XX	FT,XL		NQ,GW	LT,SO7	98,56(11)
		JA,LD(8)	XX,UE,UY		CV,ZC		DP,113
		NL,TF	LD,NQ		XY,NP		26,DV
		TF,NJ(1)	NQ,XY		NP,GW(1)		NJ,DV
		TF,XT,NJ,OB	KT,M		XY,UT		TP,39
		XX,YV	XL,XX		IX,NL		14,DW
		XY,GW	XT,UE(1)		NG,IX		113,EE(1)
		NQ,TT	NG,HC		TQ,HC		27,DP
		ZC,UE,XL	JA,LD,NP(4)		HC,IX		AP,EE,27(1)
		U,JX	XL,YV		EG,IX		
		UU,NO(6)	XA,NG		JX,U		
		UP,NJ	NL,KN		IX,AL		
		LD,NP(1)	NP,NQ		NP,YV		
		CV,XY	56,98		NL,IX,DK		
		UP,XA			JQ,JX		
		IX,EG(1)			IX,HC		
		HC,NL			NT,NY		
		UP,NJ			CV,DP		
		EG,NL			NP,NQ(11)		

* Each time period was observed on different days. For example, NQ,NP(11) means that NQ and NP were observed associating for at least five minutes on eleven days. Males were considered to be associating if they sat within one meter of each other, or if they were engaged in mutual grooming or play.

† Related males were linked by matrilineal genealogical ties.

TABLE 23

PROPORTION AND PERCENTAGE OF MALES IN EACH AGE CLASS OF EACH GROUP WHICH
WERE BORN IN THEIR PRESENT GROUP OF MEMBERSHIP AS OF AUGUST 1967

Group	Age to Nearest Year													
	1 Ratio	%	2 Ratio	%	3 Ratio	%	4 Ratio	%	5 Ratio	%	6 Ratio	%	7 and older Ratio	%
A	15/15	100.00	15/15	100.00	17/17	100.00	1/3	33.33	2/9	22.22	0/5	0.00	5/19	26.32
C	19/19	100.00	13/13	100.00	14/15	100.00	2/8	25.00	1/5	20.00	0/3	0.00	7/15	46.66
E	10/10	100.00	4/4	100.00	6/6	100.00	4/4	100.00	4/4	100.00	0/2	0.00	0/5	0.00
F	5/5	100.00	5/5	100.00	5/5	100.00	1/1	100.00	1/1	100.00	2/2	100.00	1/3	33.33
H	3/3	100.00	4/4	100.00	1/1	100.00	0/0	100.00	2/2	100.00	1/1	100.00	0/2	0.00
I	2/2	100.00	2/2	100.00	2/2	100.00	1/1	100.00	0/0	0.0	0/2	0.00	0/2	0.00
J	3/3	100.00	3/3	100.00	1/1	100.00	0/0	0.00	1/1	100.00	0/0	0.00	0/3	0.00
Total	57/57	100.00	46/46	100.00	46/47	98.87	9/17	50.29	11/23	47.78	3/15	20.00	16/49	32.65

males up to three years of age to below 50% for males four years of age and older. The high percentage of males residing in nonnatal groups may serve not only as a source of genetic exchange (Koford 1966), but may also facilitate nonagonistic social relations because males in each group have previously engaged in affectional behavior with members of different groups. The high rate of intergroup male transfer is also closely related to the extreme fluctuations in male dominance rank as opposed to that of females, since males leave one group and enter another disrupting the hierarchy on both occasions.

H. Discussion

Intergroup relations in free-ranging nonhuman primates have been described in a number of publications and reviewed by Southwick (1962) and Symonds (manuscript). This discussion, however, will be confined to a comparison of the intergroup relations at Cayo Santiago with other free-ranging rhesus monkey populations.

Observations made of intergroup relations at the La Parguera rhesus monkey colony (Vessey, in press) indicated that, as at Cayo Santiago, the dominance position of a group was correlated with size and that peripheral males were most often involved in intergroup agonistic interactions; in descending order, the frequency of other categories involved were: central males, adult females, immature males. As at Cayo Santiago, a few members of a dominant group often displaced an entire subordinate group, and no group territories were consistently defended.

Southwick et al. (1965) reported that in rhesus groups living in temples in North India, adult males normally began intergroup fights, but females and juveniles also became involved. Lindburg (1967) and Neville (1967), who studied rural rhesus monkey populations in India, also reported males to be the most active in intergroup fighting.

Lindburg (1967) has reported intergroup male transfer during the mating season along with rare intergroup copulations, indicating that in this regard, the Cayo Santiago population is not abnormal. However, the frequencies of intergroup contacts is difficult to compare, as Neville (1967) has pointed out, since the population density at Cayo Santiago is vastly greater than anywhere in India.

The findings at Cayo Santiago indicate that associations of males in the natal groups may extend into adult life and play a part in their integration into new groups, but this has not been confirmed from the Indian studies. Long-term studies of rhesus monkeys in India may clarify this point, and such studies of a single population are badly needed.

APPENDIX A

Tables 24 - 27

TABLE 24

MONKEYS REMOVED FROM CAYO SANTIAGO AUGUST 1965-AUGUST 1967

(All monkeys sent to Desecheo Island are from Group H.)

	Year of Birth	Year Removed	Destination
Males			
DI-CM	1965	1966	San Juan
132-?	pre-1955	1966	Desecheo Island
HM-31	1960	1966	Desecheo Island
JZ-37	1961	1966	Desecheo Island
CE-117d	1959	1966	Desecheo Island
S11-46d	1955	1966	Desecheo Island
ZS-CU	1964	1966	Desecheo Island
WS-AM	1964	1966	Desecheo Island
Females			
112-?	1956	1967	San Juan
41-?	1955	1967	San Juan
RB-?	1952	1967	San Juan
KA-?	1952	1965	Tennessee
XU-KA	1963	1965	Tennessee
57-?	pre-1955	1966	Desecheo Island
80-?	pre-1955	1966	Desecheo Island
AM-80	pre-1955	1966	Desecheo Island
HE-57	1959	1966	Desecheo Island
HL-80	1960	1966	Desecheo Island
CQ-57	pre-1955	1966	Desecheo Island
CU-?	1952	1966	Desecheo Island
CM-49	1959	1966	Desecheo Island
NX-RO4	1962	1966	Desecheo Island
RO2-190d	pre-1955	1966	Desecheo Island
RO4-46d	pre-1955	1966	Desecheo Island
ZF-S17	1960	1966	Desecheo Island
TT-CQ	1962	1966	Desecheo Island

Key: DI-CM means monkey DI whose mother is CM.

d = mothers are dead.

? = mothers are unknown.

TABLE 25

MONKEYS FOUND DEAD AT CAYO SANTIAGO BETWEEN
AUGUST 1965 AND AUGUST 1967

		Born	Dead
	Male		
1.	TC-EA	1962	11/1966
2.	EC-AC	1957	10/1966
3.	IU-AC	1960	8/1966
4.	JF-?	1951	11/1966
5.	KJ-128	1957	10/1966
6.	OZ-JM	1965	2/1967
7.	42-?	1955	12/1966
8.	63-?	1954	10/1967
9.	08-?	1955	8/1966
10.	- -R	1966	10/1966
11.	EP-93d	1959	10/1965
12.	HU-EK	1960	9/1965
13.	IC-EW	1959	11/1965
14.	- -CPd	1965	7/1965
15.	103-?	1952	10/1965
	Female		
16.	NC-35d	1961	2/1967
17.	BJ-AT	1958	1/1967
18.	JH-76	1960	2/1967
19.	MJ-KK	1963	3/1967
20.	104-?	1956	4/1967
21.	CD-?	1952	4/1967
22.	GC-R13d	1963	4/1967
23.	LM-94	1961	4/1967
24.	S09-92	1957	6/1967
25.	BV-64	1956	4/1966
26.	KZ-62	1965	10/1966
27.	- -DJ	1965	9/1965
28.	12-?	pre-1951	8/1966
29.	129-?	1955	3/1965
30.	UU-EW	1962	10/1965
31.	Z -11d	1960	7/1965

TABLE 26

CENSUS OF MONKEYS AT CAYO SANTIAGO, AUGUST 1965

Born 1964		Born 1963		Born 1961		Born 1959	
Male	Female	Male	Female	Male	Female	Male	Female
GROUP A							
FG-AS	FF-HS	ON-R10	OG-BLd	FA-03	*JE-11d	DK-24d	*AS-90
FJ-81	FM-41	XL-HP	XG-109	IX-ADd	*JM-106	EG-112d	*BN-93d
FL-RB	GI-119	XT-HJ	XK-BY	JX-40d	*JO-20	EP-93d	*BY-106
FT-DT	GK-BN	XX-20D	XN-62	LD-102	*JR-RB	ET-046d	nDR-07
GA-DZ	GP-LI	YV-07	XP-106	LG-81	*LB-109	EX-59d	*DT-R03d
GD-R	GS-R10		XR-37	NG-70d	*LH-EUd	TA-81	*HJ-41
GJ-DR	CT-109		XU-KA		*LI-R13d	KN-21d	*HP-31
GO-Zd	GY-64		XW-90		*LV-69d		dKA-109
GX-15	OC-HP		YJ-KZ				*KH-78d
GZ-37	WG-BV		GC-R13d				
OB-20	WR-HB					Born before 1959	
OJ-07	WY-KZ	Born 1962		Born 1960		14 55	*07 55
WI-R13d	ZB-106	TP-40d	OP-RB	HC-21d60	*HB-109	26 53	*12 pre-51
ZC-BLd	ZO-BY	UE-07	OQ-KZ	NL-29d	nHS-78d	39 54	n15 55
ZD-KH	?-R03d	UX-109	TU-R10		*IN-BV	79 54	d20 pre-51
ZH-62		UY-120d	TV-DZ		*IV-12	S05-117 57	*37 54
ZP-IV		YC-64	TW-37		* R-13d	AL-BU 57	*41 55
			UG-119		* S-15a	DV-109 58	*62 54
			UH-81		* X-85d	DW-119 58	n64 pre-51
			UI-AY		*Zd-11d	DX-R03d58	*81 pre-51
			UV-EUd				*90 pre-51
			UW-BP				*106 55
			UZ-106				*109-119 54
			ZA-EQd				*119 pre-52
							*R10-81 56
							nAY-64 57
							*BP-93d 58
							nBV-64 56
							*DZ-RB 58
							*KZ pre-55
							*RB 52

Adopted: MC, MJ, S.
Solitary males: 113, 1956; ES-AT, 1956; AN 1957.
* = infant.
? = not tatooed.

Key:
   nhCG-DMd 57 translates: cXD-57a translates:

        n = no birth this year   c = castrated
        h = hysterectomy   XD = name of monkey
     CG = name of monkey   -57 = mother of XD
    -DM = mother of CG   a = XD was adopted by 57
      d = dead (DM)
     57 = born in 1957

TABLE 26 Continued

Born 1964		Born 1963		Born 1961		Born 1959	
Male	Female	Male	Female	Male	Female	Male	Female

GROUP C

Born 1964		Born 1963		Born 1961		Born 1959	
Male	Female	Male	Female	Male	Female	Male	Female
FO-KK	FQ-38	XY-75	aMJ-KR	JD-85d	*JK-CD	CB-88	*DJ-35d
FS-KR	FV-03	YQ-KS	XB-117d	JN-KZ	nLL-105	CV-CU	*EL-112
FU-BJ	FY-LN	YW-29	XM-38	JV-R10	*IM-94	EC-AC	nHR-10d
FW-EW	GB-CD	YZ-03	YD-88		nLR-SO2	EZ-73d	*kk-55
GN-AW	GE-ND		YN-DA		nNC-35d	KT-120d	*KR-AT
GQ-AE	GG-HD		YO-112		*NF-DA	KV-129	*KS-51d
OH-KS	GH-94		YP-BX		*NK-112	KX-64	
OL-?	GL-88		YR-105		nNK-117d		
WB-NK	GR-IJ		YX-SO2		*NM-55		
WC-112	GU-74		?-AT				
WJ-L	GV-105						
WL-EL	OA-DA	**Born 1962**		**Born 1960**		**Born before 1959**	
ZK-IE	OF-75						
OL-DJ	OK-AT	TF-CH	TL-DG	HO-RO3d	*IE-EW	113 57	
L8-NH	OI-117d	TQ-RO5	TR-BJ	HU-EK	*IJ-AE	08 55	*03 55
	WZ-NI	TS-AUd	TX-74	M-20	*IK-55	27 54	*38 54
	ZG-RO5	UP-94	TY-CD		nL-105	53 55	d55 54
	ZL-BX	UT-112	TZ-38		*LN-74	63 54	*74 55
	ZT-DC	XA-35d	UB-AW		*ND-59d	103 pre-52	*75 55
	ZU-AU		UL-29d		*NH-AT	107 55	*88 55
	D9-CH		UM-10d		*UQ-R11d	S15-60d57	*94 pre-51
			UO-EW			AG-84 58	n104 56
			US-KW			AP-CU 55	*105 56
			YY-HD		(UQ=IQ)	DP-DA 58	*112-56
			K5-03			EE-58d 58	*RO5-60d
						JF 51 103	*SO2-A48d57
							*AE 51
							*AT 51
							dAU-35d 58
							*AW 51
							*BJ-AT 58
							dBU-52
							*BX-EW 58
							*CD 52
							nCH-AE 55
							dDA 52
							*DC-03 58
							*EW 52
							*HD-CD 58
							*KW-PFd 58

TABLE 26 Continued

Born 1964		Born 1963		Born 1961		Born 1959	
Male	Female	Male	Female	Male	Female	Male	Female

GROUP E

Born 1964		Born 1963		Born 1961		Born 1959	
Male	Female	Male	Female	Male	Female	Male	Female
GF-128	WP-102	XO-EA	YF-129	JA-114	*LU-EA	KJ-128	
WH-118	WQ-114	YG-24	YM-S12	NE-ED	*LW-129		
ZE-ED	ZX-24	YH-118	YS-128			Born before 1959	
ZI-S12		YT-S13	OE-ED				*24 55
ZJ-IS						95 55	*102 55
?-131		Born 1962		Born 1960		R15-33d 55	*114 56
		cNP-114	NR-24	IG-99d	*IR-131		*118 56
		NZ-131	TA-118	U-102	*IS-24		*128 52
		TB-S12	TI-129				d129 55
		TC-EA	UR-102				d131 56
		TJ-128					dAJ-102 57
		UB-115d					*EA 55
							*ED-EA 57
							*S12-128 57
							*S13-129 57

GROUP F

Born 1964		Born 1963		Born 1961		Born 1959	
Male	Female	Male	Female	Male	Female	Male	Female
FD-EK	FB-65	GW-AC	WO-DL	IU-AC	*JH-76	DS-85d	*KD-76
FP-DL	FC-K	WK-65	YB-EK	JG-EK	*JI-22		
FX-W	WT-04	YA-76	YL-KD	JS-65	*JJ-73d	Born before 1959	
WV-22	WX-76			JT-04		19 55	*04 55
ZY-AC	ZM-KD	Born 1962		Born 1960		42 55	*22 55
		NT-76			nK-73 58	R06-54d55	*65 55
		TD-65			*W-22	cCN-76 56	*76 51
							*AC 55
							*DL 55
							*EK 55

TABLE 26 Continued

Born 1964		Born 1963		Born 1961		Born 1959	
Male	Female	Male	Female	Male	Female	Male	Female

GROUP H

Born 1964		Born 1963		Born 1961		Born 1959	
Male	Female	Male	Female	Male	Female	Male	Female
FZ-49	FE-AH		UC-AM	JZ-37	*LS-80	CE-117 59	*CM-49 59
FK-RO4	FN-HT		XS-80			KP-105	*HE-57
WA-HL	WM-CM		YE-RO4				
WS-AM	WN-80		ZV-HE			**Born before 1959**	
ZN-57	ZF-S17					132 55	*49 54
ZO-97		**Born 1962**			**Born 1960**		*57 55
ZS-CU		cNO-97	NX-RO4	HM-31	*HL-80		*80 55
ZZ-CQ		cNQ-RO2	TE-49		nHT-RO4	SO11-46d55	n84 55
		NV-S17	TT-CQ		*IP-CU	BC 55	n97 55
		NY-CU	cXD-57				*?02-190d 55
		cUU-AH					*RO4-046d 55
							*S17-84 55
							*AH-49 55
							*AM-80 55
							*CQ-57 55
							nCU 52

GROUP I

Born 1964		Born 1963		Born 1961		Born 1959	
Male	Female	Male	Female	Male	Female	Male	Female
FI-116	FH-CS	MC-CS	XC-116	LT-CG	*IW-AA	IC-EW	*CS-116
ZW-CPd	WD-91		YI-AA				
	WE-AA	**Born 1962**				**Born before 1959**	
			NU-116			96 54	n91 pre-51
			TO-CPd			SO7-119 57	n116 55
							*AA-91 57
							nhCG-DMd 57
							*CPd-DMd 58

GROUP J

Born 1964		Born 1963		Born 1961		Born 1959	
Male	Female	Male	Female	Male	Female	Male	Female
ZR-SO9	WF-31		XJ-31	JQ-92	*JP-31	56 54	*31 55
			XQ-SO9		*LA-SO9	98 56	*92 pre-51
		Born 1962				121 55	*SO9-92 57
		UD-31	TN-92			RO8-65 56	

TABLE 27

CENSUS OF MONKEYS AT CAYO SANTIAGO, AUGUST 1967

Born 1966		Born 1965		Born 1963		Born 1961	
Male	Female	Male	Female	Male	Female	Male	Female
GROUP A							
L6-UV A	L5-UH	A1-HJ A	A5-RB	L7-81 A	OG-BId	Born before 1961	
M6-AS A	P2-119	C3-R10 A	B1-JE	XY-75 C	*XK-BY		
M9-BP A	P4-64	E1-JR A	C4-BP	GW-AC F	XN-62	FA-03 C	JE-11d
N6-BY A	P5-UZ	E2-LI A	E3-07		*XP-106	17 IX-AAd I	**JM-106
N8-IV A	S7-JM	E5-37 A	E4-KH		*XR-37	16 JA-114 E	*JO-20
P6-62 A	-81	F1-90 A	E7-AS		*XW-90	15 LD-102 E	*JR-RB
T2-07 A	X3-106	F2-LV A	G2-R		*YJ-KZ	21 NG-70d C	*LH-UEd
T3-37 A	U6-DR	G5-S A	G3-LH				LI-R13d
-90 A	U5-DT	G6-HP A	H6-JO				*LV-69d
T1-BN A	S8-JE	I1-DT A	OR-Zd				
X7-HP A	T4-JR	I7-119 A	N9-IV			Born before 1961	
W3-OP A	V1-KZ	OY-BY A	K6-KZ				
S3-TU A	X5-LI	J7-IN A				14 A	*07
V9-TW A	-RB	K3-81 A				26 C	15
X2-UG A	U3-R10	G4-DZ A				38 C	*20
	V7-TV					79 C	*37
	-UI	Born 1964		Born 1962		S05-117dC	*62
	V8-UW					S15-60d A	64
		FG-AS A	FF-HS	TF-CH C	*OQ-KZ	AL-BU C	*81
		FJ-81 A	FM-41	TP-40dA	*RU-R10	DK-24dC	*90
		FL-RB A	GI-119	TQ-RO51	TV-DZ	DW-119 A	*106
		FT-DT A	GK-BN	UT-112E	TW-37	DX-BO3dA	*119
		GA-DZ A	GP-LI	YC-64 A	*UG-119	EG-122dC	R10-81
		GD-R A	GS-R10	XA-35dC	*UH-81	EX-59d C	*AS-90
		GJ-DR A	GY-64	cNP-114E	*UI-AY	HC-21d C	R-13d
		GO-Zd A	OC-HP	NQ-RO2H	*UV-EUd	NL-29d C	* S-15A
		GX-15 A	WG-BVd	UP-94 C	UW-BP	NJ-EW C	X-85d
		GZ-37 A	ZQ-BY		UZ-106	IA-81 A	AY-64
		OB-20 A	C7-RO3d		ZA-EQd	KN-21d C	BN-93
		OJ-07 A				AN C	*BP-93d
		WI-R13d A				CV-CU H	*BY-106
		ZD-KH A					*DR-07
		ZH-62 A					*DT-RO3d
		ZP-IV A					*DZ-RB
		ZB-106 A					*HJ-41
							*HP-31
							HS-78d
							IN-BVd
							*IV-12d
							*KH-78d
							*KZ

Table reads as following example: caU9-BTd = castrated male U9 was adopted by female BT which acted as his mother until she died.

Capital letters A, C, E, F, H, J, I which follow the names of all males indicate the group in which that male was born.

TABLE 27 Continued

Born 1966		Born 1965		Born 1963		Born 1961	
Male	Female	Male	Female	Male	Female	Male	Female
GROUP C							
? -55 C	M1-AT	A3-EL C	B7-DC	XL-HP A	*XB-117d	JD-85d A	*JK-CDd
N1-HD C	R2-KW	B3-EW C	C6-88	XT-HJ A	*XM-38	JN-KZ A	LL-105
R4-UQ C	R3-US	B5-HD C	F5-112	XX-20 A	*YD-88	LG-81 A	*LR-SO2
S1-03 C	S2-DJ	B6-103C	F6-IMd	YA-76 F	YN-DA		*NF-DA
X8-75 C	S5-NK	B8-03 C	G1-RO5	YV-07 A	*YO-112		*NI-112
X1-94 C	T8-38	C9-IK C	H1-BJd	YW-29dC	*YP-BX		*NK-117d
U8-CH C	? -74	D3-KK C	H4-UQ	YZ-03 C	*YR-105		*NM-55
T5-DC C	W4-88	E6-JK C	I4-BX	ON-R1OA	*YX-SO2		
? -EL C	W5-112	G9-SO2C	S6-38		* -AT	**Born before 1961**	
U9-HR C	W6-BU	H2-LN C	J9-74				
? -IE C	U1-IJ	12-IE C	J3-AT			27 C	*03
U2-IK C	W9-K5	16-94 C	R1-IJ			107 A	*38
V6-JK C	U4-KK	I2-AE C	L3-KW			113 C	*55
? -KR C	? -KS		M3-ND			121 C	*74
? -LR C	V5-LL		J4-NF			AG-84 H	*75
? -NM C	59-NH		J5-NI			AP-CU H	88
W7-SO2C	? -NI					CB-88 C	94
? -TX C	W2-TZ	**Born 1964**		**Born 1962**		DP-DA C	*105
X6- ? C	W8-UL	FO-KK C	FQ-38	NT-76 F	*TL-DC	EE-58d A	RO5-60d
		FS-KR C	FV-03	NY-CU H	TR-BJd	EZ-73d C	**SO2-48d
		FU-BJdC	FY-LN	TS-AU C	*TX-74	ET-46d C	AE
		FW-EW C	GB-CDd	UE-07 A	*TY-CDd	KT-120dA	AT
		GN-AW C	GE-ND	UY-120dA	*UB-AW	KX-64 A	AU-35d
		GQ-AE C	GG-HD		*UL-29d	HO-RO3dA	*AW
		OH-KS C	GH-94		*UM-10d	M-20 A	*IE-EW
		OL-DJ C	GL-88		*US-KW		*IJ-AE
		WB-NK C	GR-IJ		*YY-HD		*IK-55
		WC-112C	GU-74		*K5-03		* L-105
		WJ-L C	GV-105		*TZ-38		BU
		WL-EL C	OA-DA				*BX-EW
		ZK-IE C	OF-75				*CH-AE
		L8-NH C	OK-AT				*DA
		ZC-BIdA	I-117d				*DC-03
			WZ-NI				*DJ-35d
			ZG-RO5				*EL-112
			ZL-BX				*EW
			ZT-DC				*HD-CDd
			*ZU-AU				*HR-10d
			D9-CH				*KK-55
							*KR-AT
							*KS-51d
							*KW-Pfd
							*LN-74
							*ND-59d
							NH-AT
							*UQ-R11d

Solitary males: ES, JV, KV, 19, DV.

TABLE 27 Continued

Born 1964		Born 1963		Born 1961		Born 1959	
Male	Female	Male	Female	Male	Female	Male	Female

GROUP E

Born 1964		Born 1963		Born 1961		Born 1959	
V3-102 E	M4-118	B2-118E	A7-IR	XO-EA E	*YF-129d	JQ-92J	LU-EA
-114 E	M8-AJ	E9-S12E	D8-LW	YG-24 E	*YM-S12	JX-40dA	*LW-129d
T6-131 E	R8-EA	F3-128E	J1-24	YH-118E	*YS-128		
-ED E		H8-102E	H7-LU	YT-S13E	*OE-ED		
-IR E			H5-114				
W1-IS E			13-IS				
T7-LU E			18-EA				
X4-LW E			F9-ED				
-S12 E			R9-S13				
V4-TA E							

		Born 1964		Born 1962		Born before 1961	
		GF-128E	WP-102	NZ-131E	*NR-24	95 A	*24
		WH-118E	WQ-114	TB-S12E	TA-118	R15-33dC	*102
		ZE-ED E	ZX-24	TJ-128E	*TI-129d	53 C	*114
		ZI-S12E		UB-115dE	*UR-102	IG-99dC	*118
		ZJ-IS E				U-102C	*128
		OW-131E					*131
							*AJ-102
							*EA
							*ED-EA
							S12-128
							S13-129
							*IR-131
							*IS-24

GROUP F

Born 1964		Born 1963		Born 1961		Born 1959	
N3-W F	M7-DL	BA-76 F	A8-W	CW-AG F	*WO-DL	JS-65 F	*JI-22
N7-76 F	N2-KD	D6-JHdF	A9-22	WK-65F	YB-EK	JT-04 F	JJ-73d
P7-AC F	P8-EK	D7-EK F	G8-AC		YL-KD		
R5-04 F	? -K	G7-DL F	OS-65				
V2-JI F		OV-04 F	OT-JJ				
			J2-11				
			K1-KD				

		Born 1964		Born 1962		Born before 1961	
		FD-EK F	*FB-65	TD-65 F		R06-54d A	04
		FP-DL F	FC-K			cDN-76 F	*22
		FX-W F	WT-04			DS-85d A	65
		WV-22 F	WX-76				*76
		ZY-AC F	ZM-KD				*AC
							*DL
							*EK
							*KD-76
							*K-73d
							W-22

TABLE 27 Continued

Born 1964		Born 1963		Born 1961		Born 1959	
Male	Female	Male	Female	Male	Female	Male	Female

GROUP H

Male	Female	Male	Female	Male	Female	Male	Female
N4-S17 H	N5-97	D2-RO2H	B9-LS			NE-ED E	
? -AH H	R6-49	D4-HE H	H9-AM				
U7-HT H		J8-AH H					
		K4-49 H					
		Born 1964		_Born 1962_		_Born before 1961_	
		ZO-97 H	FN-HT	cNO-97 H	eXD-57	BC C	*49
				cUU AH H		KP-105 C	84
							*97
							*AH-49
							*HT-RO4
							*S17-84

GROUP I

Male	Female	Male	Female	Male	Female	Male	Female
P9-CS I	P3-NU	OX-IW I	A4-CS	aMC-CS I	XC-116	JG-EK F	*IW-AA
? -AA I	R7-TO	J6-AA I			*YI-AA	LT-CG I	
		Born 1964		_Born 1962_		_Born before 1961_	
		FI-116 I	FH-CS		NU-116	96-A	91
		ZW-CPd I	WD-91		TO-CPd	SO7-119 A	*116
			WE-AA				*AA-91
							hCG-DMd
							*CS-116

GROUP J

Born 1966		Born 1965		Born 1963		Born 1961	
Male	Female	Male	Female	Male	Female	Male	Female
K7-TN J	T9-92	F4-JP J	A6-31		*XJ-31		*JP-31
K8-31 J		F7-92 J	K9-LA		*XQ-S09		*LA-S09
L1-JP J		F8-S09 J					
		Born 1964		_Born 1962_		_Born before 1961_	
		ZR-S09 J	WF-31	UD-31 J	*TN-92	56 C	*31
						98 C	92
						RO8-65 F	

APPENDIX B

A Catalogue of Agonistic and

Affectional Behavior

Agonistic and affectional behavior of rhesus monkeys has been described by Altmann (1962), Rowell and Hinde (1962), Sade (1967), and other authors. The catalogue in this appendix is modified and expanded from those found in earlier publications. It should be noted that any attempt at classification of behavior is likely to meet with limited success since observers may interpret similar behavior differently. For example, Altmann (1962) and Rowell and Hinde (1962) consider lip-smacking to be "friendly" behavior, whereas Koford (1963) interprets it as submissive behavior. Presentation and mounting are labeled as "friendly" by Rowell and Hinde (1962), but Altmann (1962) considers it to be agonistic.

Another problem of arranging behavior into categories is that behaviors that are placed in different categories may occur simultaneously in one animal. For example, submissive and aggressive behaviors may be seen together in one monkey or submissive behavior is displayed by the aggressor in an agonistic interaction while the subordinated monkey shows some aggressive patterns. Thus the catalogue presented in this appendix may be subject to a good deal of individual interpretation by the reader. I hope the problems of classification of behavior are clarified as they are examined in more detail (see Tables 28, 29, 30, and 31).

TABLE 28

AGGRESSIVE DISPLAYS AND BEHAVIOR PATTERNS

Individual Attack Locomotor Patterns

    1. Passive movement toward
    2. Supplantation or spatial displacement
    3. Interrupted run
    4. Charge
    5. Spring off tree

Cooperative Attack

    6. Mobbing
    7. Battle line formation
    8. Group supplantation, with and without agonistic display

Threat Display, Visual

    9. Piloerection
  10. Ears forward and back
  11. Open mouth
  12. Stare
  13. Brows and scalp move forward and back
  14. Head bobbing, sitting
  15. Head bobbing, standing
  16. Lunge
  17. Ground slapping
  18. Rearing
  19. Broadside display
  20. Branch-shaking
  21. Stalk and point

Dominance Display Without Threat

  22. Tail upright
  23. Male genital display from sitting position
  24. Scrotum touch
  25. Mounting with erection
  26. Mounting without erection

Fighting With Body Contact

  27. Biting of face and anterior neck
  28. Biting of dorsal neck and face
  29. Undirected biting
  30. Grabbing and pulling
  31. Hitting
  32. Pinning
  33. Push aside

Other Agonistic Behavior Patterns

  34. Scapegoating or redirected aggression
  35. Guarding of pregnant females
  36. Patrolling behavior

TABLE 28 <u>Continued</u>

<u>Aggressive Vocalizations</u>
37. Bark
38. Pant-threat
39. Growl
40. Roar
41. Shrill-bark

TABLE 29

SUBMISSIVE DISPLAYS AND BEHAVIOR PATTERNS

Locomotor Patterns

    1. Passive movement away from
    2. Jump away
    3. Run away

Postures

    4. Crouch
    5. Sexual presenting
    6. Presenting with head to the ground
    7. Presenting with head to the ground and grimace
    8. Mounted

Facial Display

    9. Eyelid flash
  10. Grimace
  11. Looks away
  12. Head flaging
  13. Lip-smacking

Other Nonaggressive, Nonaffectional Displays of
  Possible Significance in Agonistic Interactions

  14. Defecation and urination
  15. Genital stroke while being mounted
  16. Testis retraction
  17. Lose erection
  18. Fast and furious grooming
  19. Wrinkling of infant face
  20. Wrinkling of sex skin of females in first estrus
  21. Red sex skin color
  22. Displacement activities

Submissive Vocalizations

  23. Squeak
  24. Gecker
  25. Screech

TABLE 30

AFFECTIONAL DISPLAY AND BEHAVIOR PATTERNS

1. Lip-touching	6. Grooming present
2. Holding	7. Present neck for grooming
3. Comfort pat	8. Present side for grooming
4. Embraso	9. Grooming
5. Affectional present	

TABLE 31

AGONISTIC PLAY

1. Play chase	6. Stare
2. Somersaults	7. Bobbing
3. Prancing	8. "Krr" vocalization
4. Mouthing	9. Grabbing and wrestling
5. Hitting	

Aggressive Displays and Behavior Patterns

1. <u>Passive Movement Toward</u> (move toward, Sade 1967; walks toward, Altmann 1962). Altmann lists this behavior pattern as aggressive, but this is not always the case. For example, an infant or older offspring walking toward its dominant mother, or a subordinate monkey walking over to a dominant monkey in order to groom him or in other contexts may not be aggressive. However, if a monkey walks toward another monkey and that monkey responds by showing signs of submission, e.g., a grimace, then the subordinate monkey in that interaction may be said to have recognized the passive movement toward it as an aggressive act.

2. <u>Supplantation or Spatial Displacement</u> (move toward, Sade 1967; walk toward, Altmann 1962; displace, active and passive, Kaufmann 1967). Supplantation has been described as aggressive behavior and used as a criteria for dominance in rhesus monkeys (Kaufmann 1967). However, a strict interpretation of supplanting as an aggressive act and a criteria of dominance relationships may be misleading. Supplantations not indicating agonistic behavior are frequently observed. For example, an infant walks toward its mother and the mother turns and walks away, or a female walks toward a sitting high-ranking male and the male moves away from her. Therefore, every supplantation cannot be mechanically categorized as agonistic or used as a criteria for dominance. In some cases, however, supplantation is seen in the contexts of agonistic behavior and is of value in determining dominance. Agonistic supplantations are easily distinguished from nonagonistic ones by experienced observers. The supplanted monkey in an agonistic supplantation shows submissive displays and/or quick movements away from the supplanter.

Such agonistic supplantations are frequently observed and are an excellent criteria of dominance relationships.

3. <u>Interrupted Run</u>. This attack pattern shows hesitancy to make contact. A threatening monkey may run forward a few steps, then stop and make a variety of visual and auditory threat displays, then either move forward or withdraw a few steps and repeat the performance. The interrupted run rarely leads to body contact with hitting and biting.

4. <u>Charge</u> (chases, Altmann 1962; attacking run, Hinde and Rowell 1962; charge, Sade 1967). A monkey may charge another with few accompanying threat displays, particularly if it is a high-ranking male. The charge is made in a run without any hesitation on the part of the attacker and seems to be a serious attempt to make contact and engage in combat with another monkey rather than merely to threaten.

5. <u>Spring off Tree</u>. Springing off trees is seen in forested areas of the island during the context of a charge. The charging monkey runs to the side of or past the object of the charge and springs off the side of a tree either toward or away from the object of the charge. The momentum of the rebound may add to the force with which the charging monkey strikes his foe.

6. <u>Mobbing</u>. Mobbing of humans was observed at Cayo Santiago only when the monkeys appeared to be very frightened. Mobbing of monkeys was not seen at all. I was mobbed on several occasions. Once, I was following a pregnant female at dusk in hopes of seeing her give birth since blood was dripping from the vagina and the labia were beginning to separate (no births have been observed at Cayo Santiago at least since 1956; presumably they occur only at night). The female left the trail and went into the underbrush. I followed and was immediately

surrounded by a ring of eight adult males which lunged, hit and barked at me. The males hit my legs from behind and tried to grab them. As I turned to defend myself, other males at my back attacked, and I kicked them away with my feet. No attacks were directed at me above the waist, although I believe the monkeys were capable of jumping that high. I was also mobbed twice when I accidentally trapped infants alone. Since attacks by males are highly likely, two men are required to trap infants for tattooing.

7. <u>Battle Line Formation</u>. On four occasions monkeys of different groups were observed to form opposing lines of battle in a characteristic fashion. Each line was composed of three or more individuals. Both adult males and females were observed in the lines but high-ranking males stayed in back of the lines. The monkeys were not arranged shoulder to shoulder with their bodies equidistant from the opposing line. Rather, alternate monkeys would be one length ahead of other monkeys in their line so that, in effect, the line would be two monkeys in depth. As monkeys in the back portion of the line advanced, the forward monkeys either stayed in the same spot or retreated slightly so that the back-up members of the line became the frontal segment and the frontal segment of the line became the back-up members. A typical engagement of this kind is shown in Figure 6. No such battle line formation lasted more than 30 seconds. After several back and forth movements one group retreated followed by a disorganized rush by the chasing group.

8. <u>Group Supplantation, with and without Agonistic Display</u>. Smaller groups often moved out of an area before another group arrived. At feeders, some fighting and agonistic display occurred between the stragglers of a departing group (usually low-ranking) and the vanguard

FIGURE 6

BATTLE LINE FORMATION

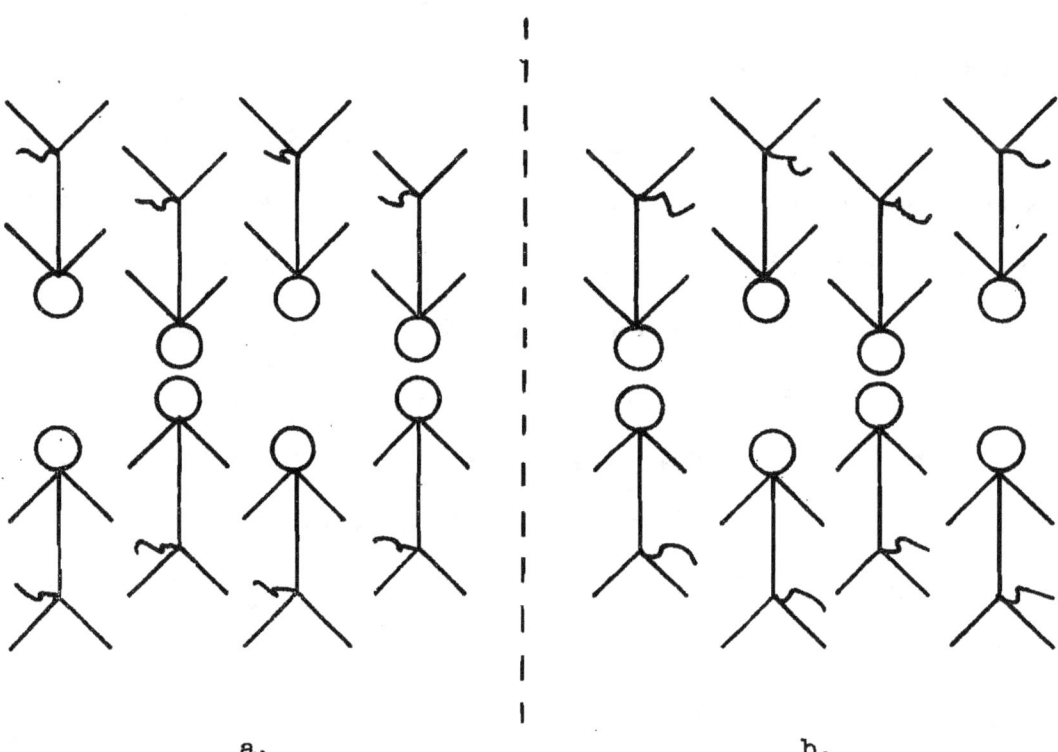

a.   b.

a.   Two pairs of monkeys are face-to-face and hit each other.

b.   The hitting monkeys withdraw and the other pair of monkeys
     move close together and begin hitting.

of an arriving group (usually low-ranking adult and subadult males and females). Such interactions are described in more detail in Chapter IV.

9. <u>Piloerection</u>. Hair on a monkey may become erect, primarily on the back and neck, either in the context of a threat or as a component of frightened submission.

10. <u>Ears Forward and Back</u> (ears-brow-eyelids, Sade 1967). A monkey may move his ears forward and back in the context of both threat and submission. If the head is lowered and raised in threat, the ears usually go forward when the head is lowered and go back or flatten as the head is raised.

11. <u>Open Mouth</u> (gives open-jawed gesture toward, Altmann 1962; open mouth, Kaufmann 1967; Koford 1963; Rowell and Hinde 1962; Sade 1967). Rowell and Hinde state that an attacking monkey may keep his mouth slightly open keeping the jaw thrust forward showing the lower incisors with the upper incisors exposed only slightly. The mouth may also be alternately opened wide and partially closed in threat.

12. <u>Stare</u> (stare, Altmann 1962; Sade 1967). Staring is a component of threat. The eyes may be opened wide and directed toward another monkey. Staring may alternate with looking away from the threatened individual.

13. <u>Brows and Scalp Move Forward and Back</u> (brows-eyebrow-eyelids, Sade 1967). The brow and scalp may move forward in a "frown" during staring and then move back.

14. <u>Head Bobbing, Sitting</u> (bobs head at, Altmann 1962; bob, Sade 1967). A monkey may make threats toward another monkey while sitting with its forelimbs extended and its hindlimbs flexed, moving its head

up and down in a bobbing motion in the direction of the threatened monkey. It may concomitantly flex and extend its forelimbs.

15. Head Bobbing, Standing (bobs head at, Altmann 1962; bob, Sade 1967). A monkey may threaten another while standing on all fours, moving its head up and down in the direction of the threatened monkey. It may simultaneously flex and extend its forelimbs.

16. Lunge (lunges at, Altmann 1962; lunge, Sade 1967). This is a hesitating charge in which a monkey may quickly move forward for about a meter, then stop short while head bobbing and making facial and auditory threats. It may or may not grade into an interrupted run or a charge.

17. Ground Slapping. A monkey may slap one or both forelimbs on the ground while standing or sitting, as part of a threat.

18. Rearing. A monkey may quickly flex and extend its forelimbs with such force that it rears up into the air. This is a component of threat.

19. Broadside Display. A monkey threatening another monkey head on may pivot on its hind legs presenting a side view and turning the head to face its adversary. Then it may pivot again to face the opponent, threaten again and then continue the pivot to present the other flank and threaten once more (see Figure 7). If the opponent is still unintimidated, the pivot may continue until the monkey is presenting his hindquarters to the formerly threatened monkey in a display of submission.

20. Branch-shaking. This has been interpreted as a territorial threat display notifying one group that another is near (Altmann 1962; Neville 1966). It was often given by a high-ranking male in the

FIGURE 7
BROADSIDE DISPLAY

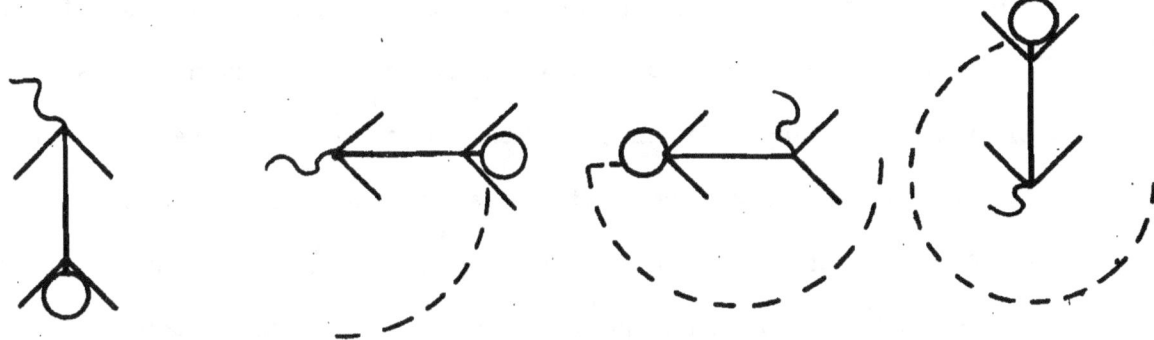

a.　　　　　　　b.　　　　　　　c.　　　　　　　d.

a.　Threat facing opponent head-on.

b.　Pivot to side and threaten.

c.　Pivot to other side and threaten.

d.　Pivot to present position.

morning near the landing as the boat approached the island. While adult males usually gave this display, females and subadult males down to yearlings were also seen branch-shaking.

21. Stalk and Point (stalk, Sade 1967). This pattern is very similar to that seen in hunting dogs pointing out game. The stalk and point was observed only in adult males and occurs as follows: A male standing on all fours seems to focus his attention toward another monkey or into the distance, perhaps at a hidden monkey. Typically, the male lowers his head for several seconds, then raises it upright for about half a second, then drops it to the lower position again. This behavioral sequence is called bobbing. Following several bobs, the male walks three or four steps, freezes again, bobs again and may flex one of his hind legs (pointing). This sequence may be repeated several times. Usually, no vocalization is uttered. The ears may be flattened or forward and the mouth open or closed. The stalk and point may or may not be followed by a charge or a run toward another monkey. Altmann (1962) and Rowell and Hinde (1962) do not include this behavior in their catalogue, but Sade (1967) does.

22. Tail Upright (holds tail erect, Altmann 1962). Tail position varied among high-ranking males. While the carriage of such males appeared to be slow and deliberate, subjectively giving them a "regal bearing," some of the high-ranking males carried their tails upright, while others did not.

23. Male Genital Display from Sitting Position. Wickler (1967) interprets the display of red genitalia by males of some species of Old World monkeys as agonistic behavior. It occurs at the edge of groups when a male is facing another group of conspecifics. Such displays

by high-ranking males at Cayo Santiago were observed commonly at the edge of their groups and were directed not only toward other groups, but also toward solitary males and unfamiliar human observers.

24. Scrotum Touch. When a male presents to another male, the dominant male may walk past the presenting male and grab or stroke its scrotum momentarily. This gesture usually takes place only if the dominant male decides not to mount the subordinate and may be a substitute for mounting to assert dominance in this situation.

25. Mounting With Erection (gives pelvic thrusts to, grips legs of, grasps legs of, Altmann 1962). A monkey may mount another monkey, either male or female, in the context of an agonistic interaction, the mounting monkey having an erection with or without pelvic thrusting. During the mating season this may lead to intromission and ejaculation, particularly if the mounted monkey is a female. Displacement copulation occurs during the mating season when a male that is thwarted in an attack on another monkey may run to an estrus female and mount her, sometimes ejaculating during the mount. A male may stop a fight between two monkeys by running over to one of the fighting monkeys and mounting it. Koford (1963a) reported that a male released from temporary captivity at Cayo Santiago returned to its group and immediately mounted the monkey directly below it in dominance rank. Presumably, this was a reassertion of dominance. However, watching a similar release at the La Parguera rhesus monkey colony, I saw a male return to his group and be mounted and groomed by a male ranking below him in dominance.

26. Mounting Without Erection (gives pelvic thrusts to, grips legs of, Altmann 1962). Males may mount without erections. Females rarely engage in mounting, but one rare instance of a female mounting a male occurred during the 1967 mating season.

27. Biting of Face and Anterior Neck (bites, Altmann 1962; bites, Sade 1967). An attacking male or female usually aims for the face and neck in "serious" combat, trying to grab the opponent's head in its hands to pull it toward the mouth. This pattern is seen in slow motion in the agonistic play of subadults.

28. Biting of Dorsal Neck and Face (bites, Altmann 1962; bites, Sade 1967). When a high-ranking male is "punishing" a low-ranking monkey during the breaking up of an agonistic encounter or when a monkey threatens a human observer, the male characteristically runs over to the offending monkey and bites it lightly on the dorsal neck region or along the vertebral column. This type of biting is usually not preceded by aggressive display on the part of the biting male.

29. Undirected Biting (bites, Altmann 1962; bites, Sade 1967). In the heat of combat a monkey tries to bite any portion of its opponent that comes into reach. However, the attacking monkey usually tries to bite the head and neck first.

30. Grabbing and Pulling (grab-hold, grab-release, Sade 1967). When a charging monkey makes contact in combat, he usually tries to grab the opponent's hair, pulling the opponent toward his mouth to facilitate biting. Generally, the aggressor tries to grab the head or neck and hold it while biting. Failing to grab the head or neck, any part of the body within reach is grabbed. This pattern is seen in slow motion during agonistic play.

31. Hitting (hits, Altmann 1962; bats, Sade 1967). Monkeys bat and hit at opponents, but since they cannot strike with much force they inflict little damage on their foes, compared with the damage done by humans and apes using similar methods of attack. The monkeys' fingers are partially flexed in hitting.

32. _Pinning_. A monkey may hold an opponent down with its forelimbs and bite it. Severe wounds may be inflicted in this manner.
Pinning is sometimes observed when a large heavy monkey attacks a
smaller monkey or when several large males attack another large male.
Fatal bites may be inflicted in the process.

33. _Push Aside_ (push, Sade 1967). One monkey may walk over to
another monkey which is sitting or feeding and push the other aside
with its forelimbs. This may or may not be accompanied by other agonistic
display on the part of both individuals.

34. _Scapegoating or Redirected Aggression_. A monkey may react to
being attacked by threatening a monkey lower in dominance than itself or
even threatening toward inanimate objects.

35. _Guarding of Pregnant Females_. Often a female, due to give
birth in a few days, is followed by an adult male or several males in
the group. Fear of the human observer during a period when the pregnant
female is relatively helpless may account for this action. The female's
movements are very slow, showing a decrease in vigilance behavior, and
she looks as if she were in a hypnotic trance staring into the distance
for minutes at a time. While she may be groomed by other monkeys, she
responds in kind infrequently. The guarding males sit near the female
and look toward the human observer. If he comes too near to the female,
the males threaten.

36. _Patrolling Behavior_. Males may pace back and forth on the
periphery of their own groups. Usually, another group is within sight
of the pacing male. Typically, a male walks 5 to 10 meters and then
makes threats in the direction of the other group. Then he walks back
to his original position and makes threats again. This procedure may

be repeated several times and may or may not lead to an attack. Rowell and Hinde (1962) describe pacing in their caged colony.

Aggressive Vocalizations

Note: I follow Rowell (1962) on agonistic vocalizations. Neville (1966) correlated the vocalization terminology of Rowell and Hinde (1962). Rowell (1962) devised a schematic diagram showing the role of these calls in agonistic display and the sonograms were presented in his paper. Since no verbal description is adequate for these calls, I merely list them. Other than the Shrill-Bark which is given as an alarm call when the group is disturbed, the context of the following calls is always in agonistic situations and they are given by both males and females.

37. Bark ("!Ho!" "repeated low", Altmann 1962; bark or snort, Neville 1966; grunt, Sade 1967).

38. Pant-Threat ("!Ho!" ?repeated low?, Altmann 1962; pant-threat or low snorting, Neville 1966; grunt, Sade 1967).

39. Growl ("!Ho!", Altmann 1962; snort, Neville 1966).

40. Roar ("!Ho!" ?repeated loud, Altmann 1962; growl, Neville 1962; roar, Sade 1967).

41. Shrill-Bark ("!Ka!", Altmann 1966; alarm bark or chirp, Neville 1966).

Submissive Displays and Behavior Patterns

1. Passive Movement Away From (walks away from, Altmann 1962; displaced, passive, Kaufmann 1967; move aside, Sade 1967). This aspect of submissive behavior was discussed in "Aggressive Displays and Behavior patterns," p. 105 (numbers 1 and 2).

2. <u>Jump</u> <u>Away</u> (hop aside, Sade 1967). In contrast to passive supplantations, a monkey may quickly jump out of the way of an approaching monkey. Jumping away is usually accompanied by submissive display on the part of the jumping monkey.

3. <u>Run</u> <u>Away</u> (flees from, Altmann 1962; flee, Sade 1967). Running away from another monkey is often on a continuum with "passive movement away from," and jumping away and is often accompanied by submissive display.

4. <u>Crouch</u> (cower, Sade 1967). A monkey may, instead of running away from an attacking superior foe, press its ventral surface to the ground, flexing its limbs, lowering its head and holding its tail as close to the body as possible. Other facial and auditory submissive displays accompany crouching.

5. <u>Sexual</u> <u>Presenting</u> (present, Sade 1962). A monkey may react to being threatened by presenting its hindquarters to the threatening monkey while looking back at it. Or a monkey may present to a nonthreatening dominant monkey, perhaps to avoid being threatened. The dominant monkey may or may not mount with pelvic thrusting.

6. <u>Presenting</u> <u>with</u> <u>Head</u> <u>to</u> <u>the</u> <u>Ground</u> (presenting for grooming, Altmann 1962). Often when a monkey presents for grooming, it flexes its forelimbs and sometimes touches its head to the ground toward the solicited animal, which is usually dominant to the solicitor.

7. <u>Presenting</u> <u>with</u> <u>Head</u> <u>to</u> <u>the</u> <u>Ground</u> <u>and</u> <u>Grimace</u>. Males, more than females, are often seen presenting with a bow while grimacing between their legs to a dominant monkey.

8. <u>Mounted</u> (mounted, Kaufmann 1967). A monkey which is mounted is usually considered to be subordinate in an interaction (Altmann 1962).

However, it was found in this study, as well as in Kaufmann (1967) and Sade (1967), that mounting was not a good index of dominance relationships.

9. Eyelid Flash (ear-eye-brow, Sade 1967). During the context of an agonistic encounter, a monkey may rapidly blink its eyelids. The white upper eyelids of estrus females, pregnant females, females that have infants less than one month old, and adult males during the mating season stand out against the bright red faces of these monkeys and are easily observed during blinking. The eyelid flash may be a partial response to a staring threat on the part of another monkey. However, eyelid flashing is also seen in threat on the part of an attacking monkey and may show ambivalence as to whether or not to attack or escape. Agonistic interactions with eyelid flashing were recorded on 8 mm film.

10. Grimace (grimaces toward, Altmann 1962; frightened grin, Rowell and Hinde 1962; grimace, Sade 1967). Rowell and Hinde (1962) give an excellent description of a grimace. "The characteristic feature here is retraction of the lips and cheeks so that the teeth are exposed and deep furrows appear on the cheeks. In the initial stages the lips are together, but the corner of the mouth is drawn back. Next the lips are parted but the teeth are not separated, the lips revealing a rectangle of incisors . . . In its more extreme form, the mouth is opened and the lips are retracted even further, the teeth and gums remaining exposed . . . With marked grinning the ears are usually flattened and the head drawn back on the shoulders."

11. Looks Away (avoids staring at, ?looks apprehensively toward?, Altmann 1962; glance away, Sade 1967). Even dominant monkeys avoid

looking at subordinates since a direct stare is interpreted as a threat. However, mothers may look at the face of their infants for several seconds at a time and the infants do not act threatened.

12. <u>Head-Flaging</u>. A monkey that is unsure of itself when threatening another monkey often alternates between staring at its opponent and looking back to see if it has any supporters. Struhsaker (1967a) interprets such head-flaging in <u>Cercopithecus aethiops</u> as an attempt to enlist support of other monkeys in an aggressive encounter. This is also the case among rhesus monkeys.

13. <u>Lip-smacking</u> (lip-smacking, Altmann 1962; lip-smacking, Rowell and Hinde 1962). This pattern is seen in different circumstances. (a) During grooming bouts it was noted that the groomer often did lip-smacking with smacking noises. The tongue may be extended from the lips and then withdrawn during lip-smacking. (b) Lip-smacking with and without grooming is seen along with other submissive displays in the context of agonistic interactions. When an infant held by its mother became frightened by another monkey or a human, it would lip-smack toward the offending individual, then immediately grab the mother's nipple and nurse, making the same lip-smacking movements used in appeasement. This suggests that the ritualization of lip-smacking may have come from feeding behavior. (c) Lip-smacking was also observed being given by high-ranking males to subordinate monkeys. The dominant male of Group A (DW) was particularly inclined to lip-smack. Typically, he would lip-smack while running between and around sitting monkeys, with his eyebrows partially lowered, his chin up and extended. The monkeys wheeled to face him, grimacing during his performance. This had the effect of calming the group, when fighting between several monkeys had broken out.

14. <u>Defecation</u> <u>and</u> <u>Urination</u>. An animal which is threatened may defecate and urinate while giving other submissive displays.

15. <u>Genital</u> <u>Stroke</u> <u>While</u> <u>Being</u> <u>Mounted</u>. When a male was mounting a male, the mountee sometimes reached back between his legs and stroked or lightly grabbed the scrotum of the mounter. Only males subordinate to the mounter were observed making a genital stroke while being mounted.

16. <u>Testis</u> <u>Retraction</u>. Males when threatened will partially withdraw their testis into the inguinal canal. This was sometimes the first sign of tension observed in a male.

17. <u>Lose</u> <u>Erection</u>. Relaxed males, particularly while being groomed, often had penile erections which would undergo detumescence if the monkeys were mildly threatened.

18. <u>Fast</u> <u>and</u> <u>Furious</u> <u>Grooming</u> (grooming, Altmann 1962; see Sade 1965). A monkey which had accidentally disturbed a resting high-ranking animal would often proceed to groom the high-ranking monkey at a very rapid rate. This seemed to calm the higher-ranking monkey and inhibit aggression.

19. ?<u>Wrinkling</u> <u>of</u> <u>Infant</u> <u>Face</u>. The wrinkling of the infant face may give the appearance of a "pseudo-grimace" and thus inhibit aggression in other monkeys. The wrinkling begins to disappear at the age of three months when the grimace begins to be seen with increasing frequency. Grimacing in infants under three months of age is rare.

20. ?<u>Wrinkling</u> <u>of</u> <u>Sex</u> <u>Skin</u> <u>of</u> <u>Females</u> <u>in</u> <u>First</u> <u>Estrus</u>. Females coming into their first mating season (at the age of two or three years) develop a pink crenulated sex skin which resembles the wrinkled face of an infant monkey. It is possible that the crenulated sex skin may, like the wrinkled face of a grimace, have the display function of

inhibiting aggression, particularly since females radically alter their dominance status at this time. From the onset of the first estrus, females usually become dominant to their older sisters. This aspect of dominance was discussed in Chapter IV.

21. Red Sex Skin Color. Wickler (1967) suggested that red sex skin color in both male and female Old World monkeys may act to inhibit aggression. This hypothesis is supported by the study of the Cayo Santiago rhesus monkeys. Redness of sex skin in both males and females is brightest during the mating season, the period of most pronounced aggression at Cayo Santiago. The sex skin of females is also at its brightest in the several weeks preceding and following parturition. During this period females are most vulnerable to attack.

22. Displacement Activities. Before and after engaging in agonistic encounters and during periods of "tension," monkeys would engage in self-grooming, digging with sticks in the ground, yawning, stretching (like that observed in domestic dogs where the chin almost touches the ground while the forelimbs are extended in front of the head). Such behaviors seemed to substitute for taking action against the monkeys or humans which were the source of discomfort.

Submissive Vocalizations

Submissive vocalizations are generally characterized by being high-pitched, whereas aggressive vocalizations are low-pitched. Rowell (1962) and Rowell and Hinde (1962) gave sonograms of submissive vocalizations of rhesus monkeys.

23. Squeak ("eee" Altmann 1962; squeak, Neville 1962; squeaks, Rowell 1962; hiss?, squeak, Sade 1967). Squeaks occur in the context of most agonistic interactions, usually by the subordinate monkey in the interaction.

24. <u>Gecker</u> ("ik, ik, ik . . ." plus spasms, Altmann 1962; geckering screech, Rowell 1962; infant gecker or chatter, Neville 1966). Infants give this vocalization when disturbed. It is accompanied by spasmic movements.

25. <u>Screech</u> ("eee," Altmann 1962; screech or scream, Neville 1966; Rowell 1962, screech; Rowell and Hinde 1962, scream; shriek, Sade 1967). A severely upset animal may utter loud high-pitched vocalizations, which appear to me to be on the louder end of a continuum of high-pitch vocalizations including squeaks.

Affectional Display and Behavior Patterns

1. <u>Lip-touching</u>. A monkey may meet and place its lips, sometimes slightly pursed, on another monkey, usually about the head. This is often followed by grooming, and the groomer has been observed to kiss in the context of grooming.

2. <u>Holding</u>. Monkeys of all ages may sit with their arms wrapped about each other for periods up to several hours during the day or for an entire night. Monkeys that hold each other are frequently associated by other affectional behaviors and spatial propinquity.

3. <u>Comfort Pat</u>. A sexually immature monkey, particularly an infant, may run to its mother and nurse or cling ventrally to her as she pats it on the back several times. This has the effect of calming the immature monkey.

4. <u>Embraso</u>. This gesture is similar to the Latin American <u>embraso</u>. Both arms are draped over the shoulders and back as both individuals sit touching face to face. Adult males and females may both initiate grooming with an <u>embraso</u>. The difference between the <u>embraso</u> and holding is that

holding extends for a long period of time whereas the embraso lasts only a few seconds.

5. Affectional Present. This is the present of the mother to an infant when she wants him to climb onto her before she moves off. The mother looks toward the infant as she presents with mild lip-smacking. Harlow and Harlow (1965) noted and described the affectional present in rhesus monkeys in his laboratory.

6. Grooming Present. One monkey may approach another closely and present, looking straight ahead away from the monkey to which it is presenting. Both fore and hindlimbs are rigidly extended, the back may be slightly arched, and the chin held up high. The grooming present differs from the submissive present chiefly in that the presenting monkey closely approaches the monkey to which it is presenting and does not look back and grimace. The monkey which presents is then groomed.

7. Present Neck for Grooming. A monkey may approach another, face it, sit down less than a meter from it, and raise its chin as high as it will go. The monkey which presents its neck in such a way is often groomed.

8. Present Side for Grooming. A monkey may approach another and then stand or sit with its side facing the other monkey. This is the most frequent method of soliciting grooming.

9. Grooming. Grooming between monkeys usually had a calming effect on their relationship. Sade (1965) gave a detailed discussion of the relationship of grooming to affectional relations in rhesus monkeys.

Agonistic Play

Most of the play behavior of immature rhesus monkeys has components of agonistic display. Agonistic play was easily distinguished from serious agonistic behavior by (1) lack of agonistic vocalization (agonistic play was usually silent except for the rare presence of a low-pitched, low-intensity "krr" vocalization); (2) lack of submissive facial displays; (3) sequences of agonistic display interspersed with other activities such as Prancing, Somersaults and Object Play; (4) rapid alternation or absence of clearly defined dominant and submissive roles in play interactions; (5) the slowing down of motor patterns involved in combat, such as grabbing, wrestling, and biting. Subadult males engage in agonistic play more frequently than other age-sex categories. Males older than four years and females older than three years play infrequently.

1. <u>Play Chase</u>. Young monkeys often chase each other back and forth taking turns chasing and being chased.

2. <u>Somersaults</u>. Young monkeys may flex their forelimbs and extend their hindlimbs quickly so as to make a somersault. This is often preceded or followed by other play activities, such as wrestling.

3. <u>Prancing</u>. Young monkeys may first rapidly flex and extend their forelimbs so as to rear into the air and then while their forelimbs are off the ground, rapidly flex and extend their hindlimbs so that the whole body rises into the air. This may be repeated and the monkeys may jump up to 1/2 meter off the ground. Prancing is often interspersed with other agonistic play patterns.

4. <u>Mouthing</u>. During play wrestling the monkeys involved usually lightly bite about the head and necks of their partners. This is the target area favored in serious fighting.

5. <u>Hitting</u>. Light cuffing is seen in agonistic play, usually during imitation of a wrestling bout.

6. <u>Stare</u>. Monkeys approaching each other to engage in agonistic play may stare at each other. Brow, eyelid, and ear movement may occur, but are not as pronounced as in serious combat.

7. <u>Bobbing</u>. Bobbing as described earlier may occur in agonistic play.

8. <u>"Krr."</u> A low-pitched low-amplitude vocalization sometimes accompanies wrestling. It was not audible at a distance of several meters away from the wrestling monkeys.

9. <u>Grabbing</u> and <u>Wrestling</u>. As monkeys mouth in slow motion they try to hold their opponent's head in their hands or to grab other parts of their opponent's body. Such agonistic mock fighting closely resembles real fighting except for the slow motion and lack of agonistic vocalization.

REFERENCES

Allee, W. C. 1951 Cooperation Among Animals, Henry Schuman: New York.

Altmann, Stuart A. 1962 A field study of the sociobiology of rhesus monkeys. Ann. N.Y. Acad. Sci., 102: 338-436.

Bernstein, I. S. 1962 Response to nesting materials of wild born and captive born chimpanzees. Anim. Behav., 10: 1-6.

Bert, J., H. Ayats, A. Martino, and H. Collomb 1967 Le sommeil nocturne chez le babouin Papio papio. Observations en milieu naturel et données électrophysiologiques.

Brown, Roger W. 1967 Social Psychology, Free Press: New York.

Buxton, A. P. 1952 Observations on the diurnal behavior of the redtail monkey in a small forest in Uganda. J. Anim. Ecol., 21: 25-58.

Carpenter, C. R. 1942 Sexual behavior in free-ranging rhesus monkeys. J. Comp. Psychol., 33: 113-142.

Carthy, J. D. and F. J. Ebling 1964 The Natural History of Aggression, Academic Press: New York.

Collias, N. E. 1944 Aggressive behavior among vertebrate animals. Physiol. Zool., 17 (1): 83-123.

Conaway, C. H. and C. B. Koford 1965 Estrous cycles and mating behavior in a free-ranging band of rhesus monkeys. J. Mammal., 45: 577-588.

Conaway, C. H. and D. S. Sade 1965 The seasonal spermatogenic cycle in free-ranging rhesus monkeys. Folia Primat., 3: 1-12.

DeReuck, A. and J. Knight, eds. 1966 Conflict in Society, Little, Brown and Co.: Boston.

DeVore, I. 1965 Male dominance and mating behavior in baboons. In: Sex and Behavior, F. A. Beach, ed., Wiley and Sons: New York, pp. 266-289.

Etkin, W. 1964 Cooperation and competition in social behavior. In: Social Behavior and Organization among Vertebrates, W. Etkin, ed., University of Chicago Press: Chicago, pp. 1-34.

Freeman, D. 1964 Human aggression in anthropological perspective. In: The Natural History of Aggression, J. D. Carthy and F. J. Ebling, eds., Academic Press: New York, pp. 109-119.

Goodall, Jane 1965 Chimpanzees of the Gombe Stream Reserve. In: Primate Behavior, I. De Vore, ed., Holt, Rinehart and Winston: New York.

Hall, K. R. L. 1964 Aggression in monkey and ape societies. In: The Natural History of Aggression, J. D. Carthy and F. J. Ebling, eds., Academic Press: New York, pp. 51-64.

Harlow, H. F. and M. K. Harlow 1965 The affectional systems. In: Behavior of Nonhuman Primates, vol. II, A. M. Schrier, H. F. Harlow, and F. Stollnitz, eds., Academic Press: New York, pp. 287-334.

Hinde, R. A. and N. Tinbergen 1958 The comparative study of species-specific behavior. In: Behavior and Evolution, A. Roe and G. G. Simpson, eds., Yale University Press: New Haven.

Kaufmann, J. H. 1965 A three-year study of mating behavior in a free-ranging band of rhesus monkeys. Ecology, 46 (4): 500-512.

_____ 1966 Behavior of infant rhesus monkeys and their mothers in a free-ranging band. Zoologica, 51 (1): 17-28.

_____ 1967 Determinants of dominance in a group of free-ranging rhesus monkeys. In: Social Communication among Primates, S. A. Altmann, ed., University of Chicago Press: Chicago.

Klopper, A. 1964 Physiological background to aggression. In: The Natural History of Aggression, J. D. Carthy and F. J. Ebling, eds., Academic Press: New York, pp. 65-72.

Koford, Carl B. 1963a Group relations in an island colony of rhesus monkeys. In: Primate Social Behavior, C. H. Southwick, ed., Van Nostrand Co.: Princeton, pp. 136-152.

_____ 1963b Rank of mothers and sons in bands of rhesus monkeys. Science, 141: 356-357.

_____ 1965 Population dynamics of rhesus monkeys on Cayo Santiago. In: Primate Social Behavior, I. De Vore, ed., Holt, Rinehart and Winston: New York.

_____ 1966 Population changes in rhesus monkeys: Cayo Santiago 1960-1964. Tulane Stud. Zool., 13: 1-7.

Koford, C. B., P. A. Farber, and W. F. Windle 1966 Twins and teratisms in rhesus monkeys. Folia Primat., 4: 221-226.

Kourilsky, P., A. Soulairac, and P. Grapin 1965 Adaptation et Aggressivité, Presses Universitaires de France: Paris.

Kummer, H. and F. Kurt 1963 Social units of a free-living population of Hamadryas baboons. Folia Primat., 1: 4-19.

Lindburg, D. G. 1967 A field study of the reproductive behavior of the rhesus monkey (Macaca mulatta). Ph.D. thesis, University of California, Berkeley.

Lorenz, K. Z. 1964 Ritualized fighting. In: The Natural History of Aggression, J. D. Carthy and F. J. Ebling, eds., Academic Press: New York, pp. 39-50.

_____ 1966 On Aggression, Harcourt, Brace and World: New York.

Lumsden, W. H. R. 1951 The night resting habits of monkeys in a small area on the edge of the Semliki Forest, Uganda. J. Anim. Ecol., 20: 11-30.

Marsden, H. M. 1968 Agonistic behavior of young rhesus monkeys after changes induced in social rank of their mothers. Anim. Behav., 16: 34-38.

Maslow, A. H. 1935 Individual psychology and social behavior of monkeys and apes. Int. J. Individual Psych., 1: 47-59.

Mason, W. A. 1961 The effects of social restriction on the behavior of rhesus monkeys. III. Dominance tests. J. Comp. Physiol. Psychol., 54: 694-699.

Mirsky, A. F. 1955 The influence of sex hormones on social behavior in monkeys. J. Comp. Physiol. Psychol., 48: 327-335.

Neville, M. K. 1966 A study of the free-ranging behavior of rhesus monkeys. Unpublished Ph.D. thesis, Harvard University, Cambridge, Mass.

_____ 1968 Ecology and activity of Himalayan foothill rhesus monkeys (Macaca mulatta). Ecology, 49 (1): 110-123.

Reynolds, V. and Frances Reynolds 1965 Chimpanzees of the Gombe Stream Reserve. In: Primate Behavior, I. De Vore, ed., Holt, Rinehart and Winston: New York.

Roffwarg, H. P., J. N. Musio, and W. C. Dement 1966 The ontogenetic development of the sleep-dream cycle in the human. Science, 152: 604-619.

Rowell, T. E. 1962 Agonistic noises of the rhesus monkey (Macaca mulatta). Symp. Zool. Soc. Lond., 8: 91-96.

_____ and R. A. Hinde 1962 Vocal communication by the rhesus monkey (Macaca mulatta). Proc. Zool. Soc. Lond., 138: 279-294.

Sade, D. S. 1964 Seasonal cycle in size of testes of free-ranging Macaca mulatta. Folia Primat., 2: 171-180.

_____ 1965 Some aspects of parent-offspring and sibling relations in a group of rhesus monkeys, with a discussion of grooming. Am. J. Physical Anthropol., 23: 1-17.

_____ 1966 Ontogeny of social relations in a free-ranging group of rhesus monkeys. Unpublished Ph.D. thesis, University of California, Berkeley.

_____ 1967 Determinants of dominance in a group of free-ranging rhesus monkeys. In: Social Communication among Primates, S. A. Altmann, ed., University of Chicago Press: Chicago.

_____ (in press) Inhibition of son-mother mating among free-ranging rhesus monkeys. Science and Psychoanalysis.

Schaller, G. B. 1965 The behavior of the mountain gorilla. In: Primate Behavior, I. De Vore, ed., Holt, Rinehart and Winston: New York.

Scott, J. P. 1958 Aggression, University of Chicago Press: Chicago.

_____ 1962 Hostility and aggression in animals. In: Roots of Behavior, E. L. Bliss, ed., Harper: New York, pp. 167-178.

Snyder, F. 1966 Toward an evolutionary theory of dreaming. Am. J. Psychiat., 123: 121-142.

Southwick, C. H. 1962 Patterns of intergroup social behavior in primates with special reference to rhesus and howling monkeys. Ann. N.Y. Acad. Sci., 102 (2): 436-454.

_____ ed. 1963 Primate Social Behavior, Van Nostrand: Princeton.

_____ and M. A. Beg 1961 Note on social behavior of rhesus monkeys in a temple habitat in northern India. Am. Zoologist, 1: 262.

_____, _____, and M. R. Siddiqi 1961a A population survey of rhesus monkeys in villages, towns, and temples of northern India. Ecology, 42: 538-547.

_____, _____, and _____ 1961b A population survey of rhesus monkeys in northern India: II. Transportation routes and forest areas. Ecology, 42: 698-710.

_____, A. Ghosh, and C. D. Louch 1964 A roadside survey of rhesus monkeys in Bengal. J. Mammalogy, 45: 443-448.

_____, M. A. Beg, and M. R. Siddiqi 1965 Rhesus monkeys in north India. In: Primate Behavior: Field Studies of Monkeys and Apes, I. De Vore, ed., Holt, Rinehart and Winston: New York, pp. 111-160.

Struhsaker, Thomas T. 1967a Social structure among vervet monkeys (Cercopithecus aethiops). Behavior, 29 (2-4): 6-121.

_____ 1967b Ecology of vervet monkeys (Cercopithecus aethiops) in the Masai-amboseli game reserve, Kenya. Ecology, 48 (6): 891-904.

Tiger, Lionel and Robin Fox 1966 The zoological perspective in social science. Man, 1 (1): 75-81.

Vandenbergh, John G. 1965 Hormonal basis of sex skin in male rhesus monkeys. General and Comparative Endocrinology, 5 (1): 31-34.

Vessey, Stephen (in press) Interactions between free-ranging groups of rhesus monkeys, Folia Primat.

Washburn, S. L. 1966 Conflict in primate society. In: Conflict in Society, A. de Reuck and J. Knight, eds., Little, Brown and Co., Boston: pp. 3-15.

_____ and D. A. Hamburg 1965a The study of primate behavior. In: Primate Behavior, I. De Vore, ed., Holt, Rinehart and Winston: New York.

_____ and _____ 1965b The implications of primate research. In: Primate Behavior, I. De Vore, ed., Holt, Rinehart and Winston: New York.

_____ and _____ 1968 Aggressive behavior in Old World monkeys and apes. In: Primates, Studies in Adaptation and Variability, Holt, Rinehart, and Winston, Inc.: New York.

Wickler, Wolfgang 1967 Socio-sexual signals and their intra-specific imitation among primates. In: Primate Ethology, Desmond Morris, ed., Aldine Press: Chicago.

Wilson, A. P. and S. H. Vessey (in press) Behavior of free-ranging castrated rhesus monkeys. Folia Primat.

Zuckerman, S. and A. S. Parkes 1938 The effects of male hormone on a mature castrated rhesus monkey. J. Anat., 72: 277-279.